THE
FAIRWAY
GAME

Edited by

DICK WIMMER

 Burford Books

The following have been reprinted with permission as noted below:

"Bobby Jones, 1923 U.S. Open" by Grantland Rice © Grantland Rice, 1954; "Jack Fleck, 1955 U.S. Open" by Thomas Bonk © *LA Times*, 1995; "Ben Hogan, 1967 Masters" and "Ken Venturi, 1964 U.S. Open" by Herbert Warren Wind © Herbert Warren Wind, 1985; "Arnold Palmer, 1960 U.S. Open" by Julian I. Graubart © Donald I. Fine, 1997; "Johnny Miller, 1973 U.S. Open" by Robert Sommers © Oxford University Press, 1996; "The Round Jack Nicklaus Forgot (1978)" by Red Smith © Red Smith, 1982; "Tom Watson, 1982 U.S. Open" by Thomas Boswell © Doubleday, 1990; "Jack Nicklaus, 1986 Masters" by Wilfred Sheed © Harper Collins, 1991; "Goldfinger" by Ian Fleming by permission, 1959; "Arnold Palmer, 1968 P.G.A." by Alistair Cooke © Arcade, 1994; "Let It Be Recorded: McQuitty Never Quit" by Mike Downey © *LA Times*, 1986; "Annika Sorenstam, 1996 U.S. Women's Open" and "Patty Sheehan, 1996 Dinah Shore" by Jim Burnett © Scribner, 1997; "Hale Irwin, 1990 U.S. Open" by Dave Anderson © Dave Anderson, 1990; "Nick Faldo, 1993 Ryder Cup" and "Nick Price, 1994 British Open" by John Feinstein © Little, Brown, 1995; "Drives and Whispers" by Dan Jenkins © Playboy, 1985; "What Was He Thinking" by Jeff Rude © GolfWeek, 1999; "Golf Dreams" by John Updike © Knopf, 1996; "Tiger Woods, 1994 U.S. Amateur" by Tim Rosaforte © St. Martins, 1997; "David Duval's 59!" by Thomas Bonk © *LA Times*, 1999.

Printed in the United States of America

10 9 8 7 6 5 4 3 2 1

Library of Congress Cataloging-in-Publication Data
The fairway game : great finishes and comebacks / [edited] by
    Dick Wimmer.
        p.   cm.
    Includes bibliographical references.
    ISBN 1-58080-039-4 (hardcover)
    1. Golf—Tournaments—United States.   2. Golf—United States—
History—20th century.   3. Golfers—United States Biography.
I. Wimmer, Dick.
GV970.F25   1999
796.352'0973—dc21   99-16952
                                                                        CIP

CONTENTS

INTRODUCTION

Dick Wimmer

"Golf is not really a game at all, but a perverse obsession designed to inflict pain on its practitioners," claims Peter Andrews in *Golf Digest*. But here, gathered together, will appear many of the joys and thrills of this worldwide frustration, or sport. Oh yes, to be sure, there is the devastating pain of Jean Van de Velde's collapse at the 1999 British Open, Dan Jenkin's spoof on TV golf, Mike Downey's McQuitty, and James Bond's strange match with Auric Goldfinger. But more often you'll encounter Jack Fleck coming out of nowhere at the 1955 U.S. Open, and such other Open highlights as Arnold Palmer's amazing charge in 1960, Ken Venturi's gritty win in 1964,

Johnny Miller's possible best round ever in 1973, Tom Watson's impossible chip in 1982, and Hale Irwin's 60-foot birdie putt that forced the playoff he won in 1990. From the Masters, there's Ben Hogan's sterling performance in 1967, late in his career, and Jack Nicklaus's stirring victory in 1986. There's the 1993 Ryder Cup, Patty Sheehan and Annika Sorenstam, Tiger Woods as an amateur, and David Duval's spellbinding 59 at the Bob Hope Chrysler Classic.

All these golden moments are nailed by the brilliant prose of Herbert Warren Wind, Red Smith, Thomas Boswell, Rick Reilly, Wilfred Sheed, and a host of others. So pull up an easy chair and join the readers' gallery, Arnie's army or Annika's air force, as you bask in your splendidly perverse obsession.

—Dick Wimmer

BOBBY JONES,
1923 U.S. OPEN

Grantland Rice

Looking back on the Bob Jones story there were, in my opinion, two critical shots in Bob's career. The first came at Inwood (Long Island) in the 1923 Open. The big ones had been escaping him—somehow—and when I saw him in New York on his way out to Inwood for a few practice rounds he was in an, "I'll give it one more try" frame of mind. Tournament golf hadn't been kind to Jones, and the 18 or more pounds he dropped during a big tournament with little but stark disappointment at the end of 72 holes had him edgy. There was something in the world besides amateur pay-as-you-go golf. At 21 he was beginning to think of law and the practice with his dad's firm.

BOBBY JONES

"You never looked better," I lied.

That '23 Open field was a roaring good one. But at the close of 72 holes, two Bobbies—Jones and Cruickshank—were tied. Cruickshank the wee Scot with the thoroughbred's heart, had come through the thickest fighting and the meanest prisoner-of-war incarceration in World War I where he served with valor as a member of the famed Black Watch. Among other tests, he'd seen his brother blown to bits right beside him in France.

When Jones and Cruickshank teed off in the 18-hole medal play-off, Cruickshank was a 10–7 favorite. Jones had "blown it" on the last hole the preceding day when, needing a sloppy 5 to win on a par 4, he blew a horrible 6. Bob didn't sleep that night. The next morning both men marched off that first tee determined to win on their own shots . . . not the other fellow's errors. That's the way it was played. Attack . . . attack . . . with but three of the 18 holes halved. On the 18th tee the match was even.

It was Cruickshank's honor. Hitting into a headwind, Bobby tried to keep the ball quail-high, below the breeze. He hit a half-topped drive that hooked into the rough. Jones' drive was long and hugged the right side, finally landing in a soft spot at the edge of the rough. Cruickshank then played the only possible shot—a recovery short of the lagoon guarding the green.

What to do? Should Jones play it safe from his own poor lie and shoot to tie the hole—and bank on wearing down his little adversary in extra holes—or would he give it the big gamble, going all-out to win or lose the title on the strength of one attacking shot? Bob studied the ball a moment before grabbing his midiron, a treacherous club even on a good lie. The club flashed back and down; the clubhead tore into the ball. It drilled straight into the swarming storm clouds, a speck of white arrowing over the lagoon and drilling onto the green 190 yards away . . . then up . . . up to within five feet of the cup.

That settled it! Bob Jones, Open champion, was on his way.

Grantland Rice is the grandaddy of all sportswriters. This piece is from The Tumult and the Shouting, *his autobiography, written shortly before he died in 1954.*

JACK FLECK, 1955 U.S. OPEN

Thomas Bonk

Forty years ago at the 1955 U.S. Open, Ben Hogan finished playing his 72nd hole at the Olympic Club in San Francisco and Gene Sarazen offered him congratulations. Sarazen then told a national TV audience that Hogan had just won another Open title.

He was wrong.

Still out on the course, back at the 14th hole, 33-year-old Jack Fleck held a golf club and destiny in his hands. Although he didn't know it, all that stood between Fleck and his unique place in golf history were five holes, two birdies, one playoff and a victory absolutely no one expected.

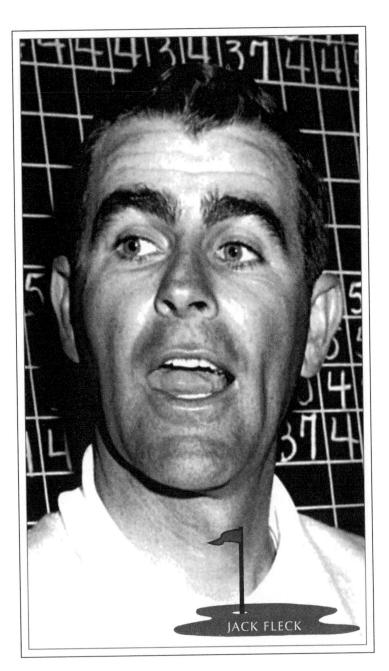

JACK FLECK

Well, there was one person who thought this virtually unknown municipal course pro from Davenport, Iowa, had a chance. It was Fleck, and he even put it in writing.

"I wrote a letter back to the late John O'Donnell of the Davenport Democrat and told him, I says, 'John, you had better get the editor to get you out here,'" Fleck said. "'There are only so many that are going to be in the running and yours truly is going to sneak in there.'"

And so he did. Playing 36 holes on Saturday in the next-to-last twosome, Fleck began with a 75, then caught Hogan, who had shot 72 and 70, with a seven-foot birdie putt for a closing 67 and forced an 18-hole playoff in what most golf experts viewed as one of the greatest mismatches of all time.

They were wrong.

Fleck, who had never won a PGA event or finished higher than eighth, outplayed the legendary Hogan, who had won the U.S. Open four times, the Masters twice, the PGA twice and the British Open once. As the gallery watched the Sunday playoff in disbelief, Fleck beat Hogan by three shots with a 69.

Fleck's professional career concluded with two more victories, the 1960 Phoenix Open and the 1961 Bakersfield Open. He retired to Arkansas and Hogan went on to the Hall of Fame.

Four decades have passed since his moment of glory, but it doesn't seem that long to Fleck, who lives about 4½ miles from Magazine, Ark. He still remembers just how he felt as he held the U.S. Open trophy.

"The satisfaction of accomplishment you get," Fleck said. "And 'It's all over! It's all over!' Team sports are a little different, but when you are out there all alone, what can anyone else do for you?"

Fleck, now 73, went it alone for a while after his wife died in 1975. Jack and Lynn Fleck had moved to rural Arkansas for her health. He remarried in 1980. Fleck still plays some senior tournaments on occasion, but he also wonders what might have happened if he had come up with another major championship, something that would have transformed his 1955 triumph from a footnote to a full chapter.

Actually he had one more chance. In the 1960 U.S. Open at Cherry Hills Country Club in Denver, Fleck finished tied for third, three shots behind Arnold Palmer.

"Had I won that it might have been a little better," Fleck said. "It might have been a little worse. We never know. We can't tell the future."

As for the past, Fleck isn't going to quarrel with winning a U.S. Open. If that was his fate, it was not such a bad one.

"Think I would have been better off by not winning?" Fleck said. "As a matter of fact, I said something to my wife beforehand, that I just hoped to play halfway decent golf to see what I could do before [Sam] Snead and Hogan retired.

"There I was. I beat Ben Hogan and Snead was five shots back. Does that say anything? I don't know. There may be something way back there in the mental."

For the 1955 U.S. Open at the Olympic Club's Lake Course, Hogan, Snead, Julius Boros and Tommy Bolt were among the favorites. The little-known pro from Iowa received scant attention.

Joe Day of the United States Golf Assn. had let the rough grow tall. Some say it was to combat the recurrence of something like Hogan's score of 276 when he won the 1948 U.S. Open at Riviera. Whatever the reason, the rough was so punitive, Edward (Porky) Oliver lost his ball after being given a free drop.

Fleck had done little to distinguish himself, although he was respected by his peers.

"Ol' Jack was pretty tough," Snead said. "He hung in there pretty good. He didn't get too excited. He kept the ball in play. That was the important thing."

Fleck had competed in 41 tournaments, most of them on the winter tour, before the 1955 Open and had won just under $7,500. He didn't break 80 in his practice rounds at the Olympic Club, but he was breaking in a new set of clubs—a new Ben Hogan signature series.

After shooting 76 in the first round, Fleck was not discouraged. He said it was because of his mental toughness.

"I was trying to compose myself and not get irritated and upset at my putting," he said. "I always called it self-composure. There were some psychologists from L.A. watching me and they said I had self-hypnosis. They were probably true. Maybe a trance is that way, I don't know."

Trance or not, Fleck's second-round 69 kept him in the hunt and set the stage for the 36-hole finale on Saturday. Paired with Gene Littler, Fleck had no problem knowing that Hogan had finished.

"I could hear the roar," Fleck said.

By the time he was at the 14th green, Fleck knew that Hogan was in at 287 and that Snead and Bolt had finished at 292. All Fleck needed was one birdie coming in to tie. Fans began joining his gallery, but Fleck immediately bogeyed No. 14 and trailed Hogan by two shots. There was no sound from the gallery.

"I remember thinking, 'Goodness sakes, they must think I'm all through," Fleck said.

They were wrong.

Fleck birdied the par-three 15th, parred the next two holes and, with the U.S. Open hanging in the balance, birdied the 337-yard, par-four 18th hole to tie Hogan. Fleck used a seven-iron for his second shot on No. 18 and lofted the ball high into the air, stopping it seven feet from the hole, then sank the putt.

Jim Murray, who was sitting in the locker room with Hogan to interview him, heard voices through a transom excitedly passing the news that Fleck had forced a playoff. Hogan didn't like playoffs, but he accepted the prospect without anger.

If Hogan had no reaction to Fleck's success, reporters were dumbfounded.

"None of us had ever heard of Jack Fleck," Murray said.

In Sunday's playoff, Fleck had a one-stroke lead going to the 18th hole, where he made par. Hogan took a double-bogey after hitting a snap hook into the left rough and taking three shots to get out.

Fleck's victory was worth $6,000. What it cost him isn't as clear. He received a 10-year exemption to play in the U.S. Open, but when the Open returned to the Olympic Club in 1966, the year after Fleck's exemption had run out, he had to qualify to play. Hogan received an invitation.

"The USA has sort of pooh-poohed my win anyway," Fleck said. "They wanted Hogan to win. He was a big drawing card. In 1966, when I had to qualify and they exempted Hogan, reporters wanted me to say something derogatory about it. A lot of them are looking for these things, you see. I wouldn't do it.

"That's life. Nobody said life is fair. Had I won in '60, maybe things would have been different. Maybe I couldn't have handled it. Maybe I would have been a sarcastic-character, like so many people that let it go to their noggin."

Fleck hasn't been to a U.S. Open since he played his last one, in 1967 at Baltusrol in Springfield, N.J. It was there that he crossed paths again with Hogan. Fleck was standing on the practice range, his back toward the tee in a group that included Ted Kroll.

Fleck heard someone call his name.

"Hi, there, Fleck," Hogan said.

Fleck said Kroll couldn't believe his ears.

"He said, 'I've never seen Ben Hogan address anybody's back in my entire life,'" Fleck said. "I've always thought that Ben Hogan was very nice."

Maybe, but 40 years ago, Jack Fleck wasn't very nice to Ben Hogan, the player almost everyone thought had won the U.S. Open.

They were wrong.

Thomas Bonk is a Los Angeles Times *sportswriter. This article appeared June 11, 1995.*

BEN HOGAN

BEN HOGAN, 1967 MASTERS

Herbert Warren Wind

For years now, golf promoters have dreaded holding tournaments in which the Big Three were not entered, but the relative quiescence of Nicklaus, Palmer, and Player at Augusta demonstrated that dullness is not the inevitable result when they are either absent or not in the thick of things. Five less publicized entrants—six if one includes Tony Jacklin, an engaging young man from Lincolnshire who showed us the best golf a British pro has produced in a big American tournament since the war—made this Masters a lively and stirring event: Gay Brewer, who won it, Bobby Nichols, Bert Yancey, Julius Boros, and quite unexpectedly, Ben Hogan, the greatest golfer of the steel-shaft era. On Saturday, in the third round, Hogan, after scoring a 74 and a 73 on the first two rounds, which is about what one looks for from a fifty-four-year-old man short on practice and hobbled with an assortment of injuries, burned up the course with a 66—out in 36, even par, and home in 30, six under. This round of Hogan's really brought the 1967 Masters to life. The fact that it vaulted him to within two shots off the leader, and thus put him in a position to pull off a miracle, was important, of course, but there was more to Hogan's round than that. Years after we had all thought we could never again hope to see this incomparable shotmaker at the peak of his powers, here he was—gray hair edging his teak-colored neck below his old flat white cap— knocking down the pins just as he did two decades ago. Oh, it was something to see! On the fourth round, he faltered early, a victim of the nerves that afflict fifty-four-year-old athletes, and was soon out of the running, but his 66 was a story in itself. I was lucky enough to be standing alongside the tenth green when he started his exciting rush down the back nine by planting a 7-iron pin-high, five and a half feet away, and tapping a touchy downhill putt into the center of the cup. It was a good-looking stroke, that putt; Hogan quickly got himself into a comfortable stance, and, somehow avoiding the long agony of freezing over the ball and finding himself unable to take the putter back (a problem that has plagued him in recent years), he dispatched the ball with little hesitation. As he walked to the eleventh tee and mounted it—it is cut deep in the woods, and few spectators cluster there—three young boys seated on the ground and propped up against a pine tree began to applaud him. Hogan gave them a broad smile that seemed to signify both amusement and appreciation, and, after groping for something to say, simply said, "Attaboy!" Then the smile came off and he got down to his tee shot. He hit a rouser far down the right side of the fairway, Position A. He drew his approach, a 6-iron, artistically. It came in dead on the pin and stopped a foot way. A second straight birdie. A third came on the short twelfth: an arrow of a 6-iron to fourteen feet and another unstuck putt. On the par-5 thirteenth, he made yet another birdie after a 4-wood to within fifteen feet of the stick and a somewhat timorous try for the eagle. A mere par 4 on the fourteenth, but a good one. Here his approach ended up in the deep swale at the front of the green, and his first putt left him a four-and-a-half-footer, but down it went, as firmly as if Billy Casper had tapped it. Then a fifth birdie, on the fifteenth, a par 5, five hundred and twenty yards long—on in two, twenty-five feet from the cup, after a well-positioned drive and a solid 4-wood, and down in two after a strong bid for the eagle. No wavering now. If anything, a crisper gait between shots. Orthodox pars on the sixteenth and the seventeenth, and then a final, masterly birdie on the 420-yard eighteenth, uphill all the way. A drive faded to fit the contour of the fairway was followed by a 5-iron to fifteen feet and another confident putt. 322 444 343 — 30. How that exhibition of flawless golf lifted everyone! Usually, when a long tournament day is over, the galleries plod for the exits tired in eye and limb, but there were no weary steps that evening. Hogan sent us home as exhilarated as schoolboys.

Herbert Warren Wind is the dean of American golf and tennis writers. He has been at The New Yorker *since 1947, was associate producer of "Shell's Wonderful World of Golf" and some of his previous books include* The Story of American Golf, The Gilded Age of Sport and Game, Set and Match. *This selection is from* Following Through, *1985.*

ARNOLD PALMER

ARNOLD PALMER, 1960 U.S. OPEN

Julian I. Graubart

It was just before 5:00 P.M. The leaders were down to their final few holes, and seven golfers still had a legitimate chance to win. Hogan and Palmer led Nicklaus, Boros, and Fleck by one shot and Souchak and Cherry by two. Dutch Harrison was in the clubhouse, enjoying his temporary perch as 72-hole leader. His one-under-par 283 would not hold up for long.

Hogan and Nicklaus moved on to 17, a taxing eight hours after teeing off for round three. With Ben's every weary step, supporters along the route shouted words of encouragement. For what it was worth, the count was now 34—he'd hit 34 straight greens in regulation. Nobody knew whether this had ever been done before. Of course, it was a statistic that would mean very little to the Hawk unless it contributed to earning him a fifth Open victory.

Hogan knew he was tied for the lead but, surprisingly, he didn't know with whom. Spotting a friend, he inquired; Palmer, he was told. Hogan was amazed. So engrossed was he in his own game that he wasn't aware of Arnold's charge. "*He's not a contender, is he?*" he replied.

Ben belted a wood down the long tree-lined 17th fairway and followed it with a strong, well-placed three-iron that came to rest about 50 yards short of the moat that fronted the island green. Nicklaus laid up, too, and his ball sat nearby on the fairway. Each mulled over his strategy for hitting to the green.

The USGA had cut the hole some 12 feet from the front of the green, insuring that birdies would be few and extremely well earned. A narrow apron of grass fell off quickly from the green to a bank that dropped a few feet to the moat. The moat separating the green from the fairway was a shallow channel about 15 feet across.

Because the green was hard and fast, a golfer would have to land his ball softly on the front to keep it close to the pin. Even at only 50 yards, trying to do so would be extremely risky. Apart from having a tight landing area, Hogan and Nicklaus would not be able to take a full swing at such a short distance; a controlled, partial swing would be needed, and this was among the toughest to execute under pressure. Nicklaus decided it was too dangerous to shoot for birdie. His pitch landed pin-high and ran 18 to 20 feet past the hole.

Hogan, deep in thought, stood behind his ball and picked out a landing spot. He was going for the birdie. A slight breeze blew in his face—a modest aid. This was his biggest shot of the tournament. He stepped up to his ball and hit a half wedge, striking the ball crisply. Arching toward the green the shot looked perfect, and applause began to build. Phil Strubing, the USA referee, saw it differently and said, "Oh, no!"

The ball came down at the top of the bank with terrific backspin. It trickled down the bank and settled at the edge of the channel on the far side. The crowd groaned. Another foot or two—maybe less—and the ball would have hopped forward and crowded the pin. Hogan walked up to the green showing little emotion. He crossed the small causeway over the moat and turned around to examine his lie. The top quarter of the ball broke the water's surface.

It was a striking scene, a panorama for a pictorial history of the game. On the putting green, Jack Nicklaus looked on, as did Julius Boros and Gary Player out on the fairway, and Arnold Palmer and Paul Harney back on the tee. Spectators whispered among themselves as they watched Hogan stare at his ball. Everything stopped. And then Hogan sat down on the bank, took off his right shoe and sock, and rolled up the trouser leg of his mustard-yellow gabardine slacks. The crowd broke into applause when it realized Hogan's intent. He really didn't have much choice, though: he couldn't afford the loss of a stroke by taking a drop. He was going to splash it out and hope to get it close enough to save par.

Ben stepped down the bank and placed his bare foot into the cool water. The footing was slippery, so out he came to put on his shoe without the sock. Back down he went. This time, satisfied with his stance, he lashed into the ball, and out from a fountain of spray it hopped onto the green. Newspaper reports of the distance the ball rolled past the hole ranged from 4 to 20 feet. Whatever, all observes agreed: Hogan's par putt never had a chance. Stunned, he left the hole tied with Nicklaus, who barely missed his birdie putt.

Next came Boros, who made his own unsuccessful crack at birdie on 17. Then, facing a three-footer for par, he missed the putt and fell two strokes behind Palmer.

Hogan and Nicklaus both seemed spent. The 17th hole had taken a lot out of the kid as well as the veteran. Nicklaus acknowledged in his 1969 book, *The Greatest Game of All*, that his concentration was gone and that he assumed mistakenly that he was out of the tournament. In fact, a birdie would get him, and Hogan for that matter, back to four-under-par 280, forcing Palmer, who was then on the 17th fairway, to birdie one of the final two holes to win outright. Both golfers were shaky, but still in contention on the 18th tee.

Jack choked up on his driver, trying to fade the ball safely onto the fairway, but he pushed it and it landed in the right rough. Ben took the opposite approach. Trying to cut as much distance off the uphill second shot as possible, he navigated the shortest route to the green. Almost the entire flight of his ball would be over water—and there would be no pitching out of this hazard. He selected a landing spot that would give him the best possible approach shot.

His ball exploded off the clubface, as on all his drives, but this one he hooked slightly. It was going to be close. Just before reaching land, it dove into the pond, a foot short of the opposite bank. It was all over now. Walking up the fairway, young Nicklaus looked across at the great Hogan. All life seemed to have gone out of him.

Jack hit a four-iron into the rough to the right of the green. He now had a very difficult chip from near the scorer's tent. He played it wonderfully well, leaving himself some six feet below the pin. He didn't think it really mattered, but if he could sink this par putt it could tighten the screws on Palmer at the home hole. Nicklaus missed it. He finished at two-under-par 282, one shot better than Dutch Harrison.

Hogan's finish at 18 was painful to watch. It was reminiscent of his 1955 U.S. Open play-off against Jack Fleck, when he lost his footing on his final tee shot and then couldn't dig his ball out of the appallingly high Olympic rough. Only this time he didn't conclude on a long, long putt that carried a hint of defiance. At Cherry Hills he hit his fourth shot over the green, chipped on in five, and two-putted—once lifting his head while putting and topping the ball. Thinking 279 only moments earlier on the 17th fairway, he finished with a bogey six and a triple-bogey seven for an even-par 284.

At 18, Boros needed a birdie to get back to three under, a score that would give him a chance, albeit slim, to make a play-off. But Julius landed in a bunker and bogeyed his second straight hole. He finished at one-under 283.

Three men still chased Palmer: Souchak, Fleck, and Cherry.

Arnold did not receive confirmation of Hogan's bogey at the 17th hole until after he had hit his second shot there. "You mean I'm leading the tournament all alone?" he asked, surprised and delighted. "Well, now it's a different story." His layup had settled a few yards farther way from the green, and farther to the left, than Hogan's. He was taking no chances now, and his wedge carried some 30 feet beyond the hole. He coolly two-putted for his par to remain at four under.

One more par, just one more par—that's what he wanted at 18. He had a two-stroke cushion over Nicklaus and over Souchak, who had just parred number 16. Fleck, now playing the 16th, was his closest pursuer, just one stroke behind. Cherry, back on the 15th hole, faced a two-stroke deficit.

Palmer hit a one-iron from the 18th tee across the pond and safely onto the fairway. His second shot, a four-iron, came up short and to the left of the green. He was 80 feet from the pin and in the rough. If he took three to get down, one of his pursuers might still catch him. If he got down in two, he'd have his 280, and somebody would have to get hot to catch him. This was the moment he'd waited for all his golfing life.

Arnold hit the perfect chip shot. It ran up two and a half feet of the pin. Walking to his ball, he casually repaired a ball mark, then surveyed his line. When he bent over his ball to putt, he said later, it seemed like a 25-footer. In the long shadows of the late Denver afternoon, Arnold Palmer rolled it home. He took two quick steps forward, scooped it up out of the cup, and without breaking stride he peeled off his red sun visor and pitched it high in the air toward the gallery at the back of the green. Palmer, beaming, looked like some happy kid half his age. On NBC's videotaped broadcast, an announcer cried, "Palmer has won! Palmer has won!"

The last of the ten contenders had made his final bid. One by one, nine of them had fallen away. Palmer, with his final-round 65, had overtaken 14 players to capture the 1960 U.S. Open. His seven-shot comeback to win was the largest ever. His 65 was the best finish by an Open champion, one stroke better than Gene Sarazen's concluding score in 1932. His 280 was the second lowest winning score in Open history. Speaking with his wife, Winnie, on the phone after the press conference, Arnold skipped the details, "Hi, ya, lover. We won."

Julian I. Graubart has written for Golf Journal *and numerous health publications.* Golf's Greatest Championship: The 1960 U.S. Open *was published in 1997.*

KEN VENTURI, 1964 U.S. OPEN

Herbert Warren Wind

*H*ad it not been for his remarkable victory in the United
States Open in 1964, Ken Venturi might well have been remembered as the brilliant young player who had three times come
tragically close to winning the Masters—in 1956, 1958, and
1960. In the early 1960s, beset by injuries, he almost faded from
sight. Just before the 1964 U.S. Open, he suddenly began to
look like the Venturi of old. How he won the Open at Congressional is one of the most inspiring stories in American golf.

There is no question at all in my mind but that the 1964
United States Open Championship, which Ken Venturi won

KEN VENTURI

last month at the Congressional Country Club in Washington, will be remembered as one of the greatest Opens. Such an assertion takes in a good deal of territory, I know, because over the years since 1895, when ten professionals and one amateur teed off in the inaugural U.S. Open, the national championship has, far more often than not, produced climaxes that have outfictioned fiction. Probably no Open can ever match the 1923 championship at the Country Club, in Brookline, Massachusetts, when Francis Ouimet, then an unknown twenty-year-old amateur up from the caddie shack, tied the regal British professionals Harry Vardon and Ted Ray and then went on to defeat them in a three-man playoff, but that is the only Open I would consider more stirring than the one that has just taken place. I am not for a moment forgetting the 1960 Open, at Cherry Hills, near Denver, when Arnold Palmer came dashing out of nowhere to birdie six of the first seven holes on his final round and go driving on to a 65 and victory—or, to cite just one more example, the 1950 Open, at Merion, outside Philadelphia, which Ben Hogan captured only sixteen months after an all but fatal auto accident had made it extremely doubtful whether he would be able to walk again, let alone be a force in competitive golf.

The 1964 Open was notable for much more than a powerful third act. From the morning of the first round, when Sam Snead, the ablest golfer who has ever won our national championship, insured his twenty-fourth failure in the event by four-putting the fourth green and then three-putting the sixth (after which he flung his ball in disgust into a convenient water hazard), the tournament was charged with exceptional golf and exceptional human interest, and both kept building until we were presented with the improbable spectacle of a winner emerging from golf's deepest limbo to stagger ashen-faced down the long incline to the final green after beating off not only his last challengers but the threat of heat prostration.

To my knowledge, there has never been anything like this in golf history.

A hundred and fifty qualifiers started the Open this year, as usual, but the championship is really the story of three players—Venturi, Palmer, and Tommy Jacobs. Thursday, the day of the first round, belonged almost completely to Palmer. He was a comparatively late starter, going off at twelve-twenty-five, when two-thirds of the field were out on the course or already back at the clubhouse. One of the first men out, Bill Collins, who had the advantage of shooting to greens that hadn't yet been baked hard by the fierce sun, had succeeded in matching par—70—but in general the scores were running high, and so was the feeling among the golfers that once again an Open course had been made a bit too severe. For a change, the chief complaint was not that the United States Golf Association, which conducts the Open, had narrowed the fairways too drastically and allowed the rough to grow impossibly high and lush; in fact, it was agreed that the fairways were wide almost to the point of generosity and that the rough, emaciated by a prolonged dry spell, was eminently playable. Since there was also a minimum of fairway bunkering, Congressional undoubtedly constituted the easiest examination in driving of any Open course in at least a decade. What, then, was giving everyone so much trouble? Well, a number of things. To begin with, Congressional, at 7,053 yards, was the longest course in Open history, and some of the Brobdingnagian par 4s—particularly two holes that are ordinarily played by the club members as par 5s but had been converted into par 4s for the championship—were breeding all kinds of bogeys. On these holes, some of the shorter hitters were unable to reach the greens with two woods, and the longer hitters, who could get home with an iron, found that their low-trajectory approaches were bounding off the greens. Another complaint—and again a legitimate one—was that the greens, a blend of grasses known as Arlington Bent and Congressional Bent, were exceedingly grainy. On long approach putts against the grain, it took a real rap to get the ball up to the hole, and on sidehill putts it was hard to judge how much to allow for the break—sometimes the ball didn't break at all.

Just when the conviction was setting in that, under the existing conditions, no one would be able to score below 70, Palmer went out and brought in a 68. He was not in his most impressive form, either—especially on the first nine, where he hooked several drives badly. Palmer is a resourceful scrambler when he has to be, though, and he bailed himself out of trouble with deft chipping and putting until he got his driving under control. He paced himself shrewdly, picking up his birdies on the short drive-and-pitch par 4s, and coming through with his best tee shots on the long par 4s, where his tremendous power enabled him to play his approaches to the hard greens with lofted medium irons. (For example, on the thirteenth, 448 yards long and with the green lying at the top of a fairly steep rise, he got home with a 5-iron on his second.) Still, his most conspicuous assets were, as usual, his huge confidence and poise. Whereas the awareness of participating in an important championship like the Open rattles most players, even the seasoned ones, Palmer thrives on the pressure, the crowds, the noise—the whole charged-up atmosphere. As he put together his 68, to take a two-shot lead, he seemed more relaxed than a man strolling around his own back yard, and one got the feeling that he might very well be on his way to repeating his classic performance in the Masters last April, when he jumped into a tie for the lead on the first day and then pulled farther and farther away.

Friday, the day of the second round, was humid and breezeless, with the temperature hovering around ninety, but the course played a shade more easily, because, for one thing, a rainstorm shortly after daybreak had taken some of the starch out of the greens. For another thing, a threat of more rain during the day had prompted the officials to place the pins in high spots that would drain well and were less exacting targets. Palmer, one of the earlier starters, reached the turn in 34, one under par. He was playing very well. When he rolled in a curving thirty-five-footer for a birdie 3 on the tough thirteenth, to go two strokes under par for the round and four strokes under par for the tournament, it looked as if he would be holding such a comfortable lead at the end of the first thirty-six holes that on Saturday, when both the third and the fourth rounds would be played, a pair of steady, unfancy 72s would be all he would need to wrap up his second victory in the Open.

Only one other player was making any substantial headway against par. This was Tommy Jacobs, a twenty-nine-year-old Californian who was appearing in his seventh Open. One of the most mature young men on the professional circuit, Jacobs is quite an interesting golfer. Essentially more of a swinger than a hitter, he has a tendency to become a little erratic when the tempo of his swing goes awry, but he can get awfully hot, particularly on long, punishing courses. He plays a much bolder game than most of his all too odds-conscious colleagues, and, in addition, he has streaks when he holes putts from all over the greens. On his first round at Congressional, Jacobs had been two strokes under par after the first eleven holes, only to finish weakly with four bogeys on the remaining seven holes, for a 72. On his second round, playing two threesomes in front of Palmer, he was once again two under par after eleven holes, but this time, instead of faltering, he started to take Congressional apart as if it were a hotel course in Switzerland. Having birdied the thirteenth just before Palmer did, he proceeded to birdie the fourteenth, by planting a 6-iron approach five feet from the cup, and then birdied the par-5 fifteenth with a fourteen-foot putt. This burst put him five shots under par for the first fifteen holes, and spectators from all over the course, including a few Palmer men on detached service from what is known as Arnold's Army, raced to the sixteenth hole to see if Jacobs could hold on the rest of the way. Jacobs occasionally becomes a bit nervous under the strain of competition, but there was not the slightest suggestion of tension about him as he parred the next two holes and then confronted the eighteenth, a par 4 an intimidating 465 yards long, on which the last four hundred yards of the fairway sweep down to a thumb-shaped green that juts well out into a sizable pond. After driving down the left side of the fairway, Jacobs, rejecting a more cautious shot, fired a 5-iron right at the pin. The ball had perfect line, but after plummeting down onto the front edge of the green it stopped dead, a full sixty feet from the cup. Jacobs stepped up and coolly holed that monstrous putt. His 64 did several things. It gave him a halfway-mark total of 136 and catapulted him into the lead, a stroke in front of Palmer, who added a splendid 69 to his opening 68. It equalled the record low score for an Open round, set by Lee Mackey, Jr., at Merion in 1950. (Mackey, incidentally, had an 81 on his next round.) It demonstrated that Congressional, like the first-class course everyone was beginning to realize it was, required excellent golf but would yield to brilliance. Furthermore, as all the facts of Jacobs' round became known—that he had missed the fairway only twice with his tee shots, for example, and that in hitting all but two of the greens on the regulation stroke he had eleven times put his approach twenty-feet or less from the pin—there was much speculation as to whether his 64 might not be the finest round ever played by a man in serious contention in a major championship. For my part, I would place it ahead of Palmer's 65 in 1960 at Cherry Hills, Gene Sarazen's 66 in 1932 at Fresh Meadow, on Long Island, and Henry Cotton's 65 in the 1934 British Open at the Royal St. George's, in Sandwich, for all three of those courses were far less demanding than Congressional. Indeed, Hogan's 67 in

1951 at Oakland Hills, near Detroit, is the only round that seems to me to be in a class with Jacobs' 64. (It should, however, be noted that Palmer's 65, Sarazen's 66, and Hogan's 67 all came on the fourth round and carried all three to victory.)

Ever since 1898, when our Open, taking its cue from the older British Open, was extended to seventy-two holes, the final thirty-six have been played in one day. Once, most seventy-two-hole tournaments were set up this way, but in the years after the Second World War there was a trend to a less demanding (and more lucrative) arrangement—one that called for four days of play, with a single round each day. Today, the Open is the only tournament of any consequence in this country that still adheres to the climactic double round. It does so because the United States Golf Association remains convinced that endurance as well as skill should be a requisite of a national champion. Certainly only the soundest swings can stand up under the attribution of thirty-six holes in one day, and that is what the U.S.G.A. has in mind when it speaks of endurance. On Saturday morning at Congressional, however, with the temperature climbing into the nineties, it was apparent that sheer physical endurance would also be necessary. For this reason, most veteran observers felt that Palmer, who is probably the strongest man in golf, would outlast and outplay Jacobs. Another point in Palmer's favor was that the two leaders were paired, as is customary on Open Saturday, and it was thought that Jacobs would find the stress of a head-to-head duel harder to take than Palmer. No other golfer was given more than an outside chance of catching the front-runners. The nearest man, Collins, stood at 141, four shots behind Palmer and five behind Jacobs. Venturi and Charlie Sifford, the outstanding Negro professional, were next, at 142.

The first surprise of the long, scorching day was Palmer's rocky start. Obviously impatient, he went aggressively for the pin on his approaches from the very first hole. Despite the fact that the greens had been soaked by a heavy rain during the night and were holding well, these were questionable tactics — or at least they seemed so after Palmer missed the first five greens. He hit the sixth, but when he then three-putted it, he fell four shots behind Jacobs, who was playing placidly and well. At this point, a third man most unexpectedly entered the picture — Venturi. Paired with Ray Floyd two twosomes in front of Palmer and Jacobs, Venturi had birdied the eighth at about the time Palmer was three-putting the sixth. It was his fourth birdie of the day. He had begun his rush on the first green, when his ten-foot putt for a birdie had hung on the lip of the cup for almost a minute and then toppled in. After that happy augury, he had gone on to birdie the fourth, the sixth and the eighth and to par the other holes, and so, as he moved with his habitual splay-footed stride down the ninth fairway, wearing his habitual white cap and frown of concentration, he was no longer on the periphery of contention, he was in the thick of it. He had actually overtaken and passed Palmer.

The ninth hole, a par 5 measuring 599 yards, is the longest hole at Congressional. It is called the Ravine Hole, because, about a hundred and ten yards from the green, the fairway, after ascending a gentle hillside, plunges abruptly down some forty feet and then rises as sharply to a relatively small, well-trapped green. It is doubtful if any player in the field could have reached the ninth green in two shots, and, in any event, no one was of a mind to try it; on both banks of the ravine, the fairway had been allowed to grow up into rough, so there was nothing to be gained by taking the gamble. The sensible way to play the ninth, and the way every man in the field attempted to play it, was to lie up short of the ravine on the second shot (usually with a long iron) and hope to put the third shot close enough to the pin to have a crack at a birdie. On his third round, Venturi did precisely this, punching his third, a firm wedge shot, eight feet from the pin. He got the putt down to reach the turn in 30, five shots under par. (His irons to the green had been so accurate that his score could have been even lower; he had missed holeable birdie putts on both the third and the seventh greens.) Venturi kept on going. After getting his pars on the tenth and eleventh holes, he hit what was possibly his best iron shot of the morning on the 188-yard par-3 twelfth—a full-blooded 4-iron, which stopped hole-high about sixteen feet to the left of the pin. He played the sidehill putt to break down some three inches, and it fell into the middle of the cup. That birdie put Venturi six under par for the round and four under par for the tournament. A glance at a nearby scoreboard brought the news that Jacobs had meanwhile bogeyed both the eighth and the ninth and was now only three under par for the distance. It was hard to believe, but it was a fact: Venturi was leading the Open.

If any golfer in the field had swept to the front on Saturday in such a fantastic fashion, his surge would naturally have excited the galleries at Congressional, but the fact that it was Ken Venturi who was working this miracle made the air incalculably more electric. Venturi's rapid rise to fame and subsequent tumble back into obscurity are familiar to all who follow golf. The son of the manager of the pro shop at the Harding Park public course, in San Francisco, he first achieved national recognition in 1953, when, a slim, handsome twenty-two-year-old amateur, he was selected for our Walker Cup team. In 1956, still an amateur after completing a tour of duty in the Army, he confounded the golf world by decisively outplaying the whole field in the first three rounds of the Masters at Augusta and entering the final round with an authoritative four-stroke lead. Then he shot a jittery 80, and lost the tournament by a stroke. It should be remarked, I think, that his play on that last round was not the utter collapse it has since been called, for he hit no really bad shots; rather, he kept missing the greens on his approaches by small margins, and he failed to hole any of the five- and six-foot putts that his chips left him. In two subsequent years, he came very close to winning at Augusta. In 1958, when Palmer first broke through in the Masters, Venturi, who was paired with him on the final round, was only a shot behind as they entered the stretch, but Palmer shook off his challenge by making a memorable eagle on the thirteenth. In the 1960 Masters, Venturi fought his way back into the battle after a spotty first round, and had the tournament apparently won when Palmer, the only man he still had to worry about, caught him by birdieing the seventy-first hole and beat him by birdieing the seventy-second.

After this third disappointment in the Masters, something went out of Venturi's game, and in a relatively short time it was apparent that he was no longer the superb golfer he had been between 1956, when he turned professional, and 1960. In those days, he had been not only one of the leading money-winners on the professional tour but probably the most proficient shotmaker in the country. I believe that the Venturi of that period was the finest iron-player I have ever seen—not excepting Byron Nelson, Venturi's teacher. Venturi's style with the irons was not particularly graceful. He took the club back in an upright arc with three rather distinct segments to it, but he arrived at the top of his backswing with his hands in an ideal position and his body perfectly balanced, and it seemed that all he had to do then in order to come into the ball just as he wanted to was to move his hips a notch to the left at the start of the downswing. Moreover, he possessed a rare instinct for iron play; he adapted his shots not only to the wind and the weather but also to the terrain he was playing from and playing to. For example, he would feather one approach in to the flag with a little left-to-right drift and burn his next approach in low and hard and dead on the target. By 1961, though, as I say, he was no longer playing golf of this calibre, and in the succeeding years his game continued to disintegrate. A succession of physical ailments, ranging from a back injury to walking pneumonia, contributed to this decline, but even when Venturi was feeling fit he played unimpressively. His confidence seemed completely shot. He failed to qualify for the Open in 1961, 1962, and 1963, and last year his total winnings on the professional tour came to less than four thousand dollars. This spring, he suffered the crowning humiliation of having to watch the Masters at home on television, because he had not qualified for an invitation to the 1964 tournament.

Venturi's behavior during his protracted ordeal was exemplary, and it won him the admiration of his fellow-professionals. He never bellyached about his lot, he was not envious of his friends' successes, and he quietly kept trying to put his game together again. This display of character came as a surprise to a number of people around golf. As a young man and one of Hogan's heirs presumptive, he had shown himself to be pleasant and very likeable, but, perhaps because his honors had come to him so quickly and easily, there seemed to be large areas in which he lacked perception and tact. After a low round at Augusta, for example, he would come sweeping up the stairs of the clubhouse, the reporters and photographers at his heels, and, sailing by the likes of Hogan and Snead, he would scale his cap halfway across the players' lounge as if he owned the world. He was not arrogant, though; he was simply very young. In adversity, he grew up, and revealed himself as a man of fibre. Late this spring, he suddenly began to play quite well again. In June, in the two weeks preceding the Open, he tied for third in the Thunderbird Open and then tied for sixth in the Buick Open. Though his putting stroke remained somewhat unsound, which it always had been, and though he hit a few wild shots in each round, he was setting himself up far more comfortably before the ball than he had done in years, he was playing with a new vigor, and he was concentrating well.

At Congressional, I watched a good part of Venturi's first two rounds, for, like everyone else, I wanted very much to see him do well. His opening 72 could easily have been several shots higher, for he played a number of holes very loosely. He topped one bunker shot cold, fluffed another bunker shot completely, and, on a hole where his heeled drive wound up deep in the rough, did not even reach the fairway with his recovery. On his second round, he played much more surely, en route to a 70. Early in the round he sank a few bothersome putts, which did his morale a great deal of good, and he was rifling his irons like the Venturi of old. At the same time, not even his warmest supporters would ever have dreamed that on Saturday he would have the shots, the fire, and the emotional composure to birdie six of the first twelve holes and go out in front.

Venturi did not stay out in front very long. Jacobs, summoning up some fine attacking shots, played the second nine in 34—one under par—to post a 70 and a fifty-four-hole total of 206. Venturi, after taking a 36 in for a 66, stood at 208. Near the end of the morning round, he had wavered discernibly. On the seventeenth green, he had missed a putt of just eighteen inches, and on the last green he had missed one of thirty inches, in both cases also missing his par. We could only give him all credit for his gallant dash and conclude that apparently he had just run out of gas. Perhaps, after all, that was inevitable for Venturi. Strangely, everyone at Congressional, I think, felt a bit better about things when, shortly after he returned to the clubhouse at the luncheon interval, it was announced that he had been near collapse from the heat on the last five holes. His seemingly imminent failure could at least be attributed to forces beyond his control. On the advice of a doctor, he spent the bulk of the fifty-minute interval resting. He drank some tea but ate no solid food. Then he took some salt tablets and headed for the first tee, accompanied by the doctor, who walked the final round with him.

The leaders had hardly begun the final round when, for the first time in hours, Palmer got back into the picture. In the morning, harried by his wretched putting, he had never really recovered from his poor start and had ended up with a 75, giving him a total of 212 at the three-quarters mark and putting him six shots behind Jacobs and four behind Venturi. All morning long, Palmer had not made a single birdie, but he started his afternoon with a flamboyant one. Jacobs then double-bogeyed the par-3 second, after pulling his tee shot into deep trouble, and Palmer closed to within three shots of him. It now looked very much as if we might be seeing one of Palmer's patented whirlwind finishes. However, it became clear, tardily, that the significant thing about Jacobs' double bogey was that it had thrust Venturi back into a tie for first. Playing two holes ahead of Palmer and Jacobs, Venturi looked drawn and pale, and he was walking slowly on stiff, old man's legs, but he was executing his shots with poise and hitting the ball with an astonishing sharpness. He came to the ninth, the 599-yard Ravine Hole, after parring seven of the first eight, still tied for the lead with Jacobs.

I arrived at the ninth too late to see Venturi play his drive or his second shot. His drive must not have been very long, for, I was told, he played a full 1-iron on his second. What a shot that must have been! There was his ball sitting up in the middle of the fairway a mere five yards from the edge of the ravine. Only an extremely confident golfer would have attempted to lay up so daringly close to the brink and as I gazed at the ball it occurred to me for the first time that Venturi could win the Open. In any event, that audacious 1-iron put him in position to birdie the hole. The flag was set far to the back of the green, so that there was a menacing trap only about twenty feet directly behind it, but Venturi went for the pin and stopped his wedge nine feet past it. Faced with a delicate downhill putt that broke to the left, he played it exactly right; his ball caught the high corner of the cup and spun in. When it dropped, I felt for the first time that Venturi *would* win the Open. With this beautifully engineered birdie 4, he had regained the undisputed lead, and, as it turned out, he not only held on to it the rest of the way but widened it—eventually to four strokes—for he played par golf in, and both Jacobs and Palmer, forced to gamble at this stage of the game, ran into a succession of bogeys.

Indeed, after the ninth it became increasingly evident that only the possibility of physical collapse stood between Venturi and victory. The sun was still beating down furiously, and on the fourteenth hole, where he had started to wobble in the morning, his slow walk decelerated into a painful trudge and his head began to droop. Into my mind's eye, as I watched him, came a photograph from old sports books showing Dorando Pietri, the little Italian marathon runner, being helped by his countrymen across the finish line in the 1908 Olympic Games after he had crumpled in exhaustion only a few yards from his goal. Venturi hung on tenaciously, however, and while he hit at least one very tired shot on each hole after that, some fortunate bounces and his own tidy work around the greens saw him safely through to the eighteenth hole, the long par 4 sloping gradually down to the peninsula green. He needed only a 7 there to win. His tee shot was weak but straight. He blocked out his 5-iron approach to the right, away from the water, and went into a bunker about forty yards from the pin. He played a much braver recovery than he had to—a beautiful, floating wedge shot that sat down ten feet from the cup. He holed the putt. He had done it.

While I think that the thousands encamped the length of the eighteenth fairway will always treasure that moment when Venturi walked triumphantly off the final green, a champion at last, I am sure they would agree with me that the Open reached its dramatic peak a few moments earlier, when, after hitting his second shot, he came walking shakily down the long slope. He was going to make it now, he knew, and in response to the tumultuous ovation he received as he descended the hill he removed his cap, for the first time that day. A little sun would not hurt now. I shall never forget the expression on his face as he came down the hill. It was taut with fatigue and strain, and yet curiously radiant with pride and happiness. It reminded me of another unforgettable, if entirely different, face—the famous close-up of Charlie Chaplin at the end of *City Lights,* all anguish beneath the attempted smile. Venturi then put his cap back on and hit those two wonderful final shots.

Few things repair a man as quickly as victory. At his press conference back in the air-conditioned clubhouse Venturi, who has a bright wit, made a number of trenchant remarks. Since we live in an age when every golf hero's band of supporters bears a catchy alliterative name, such as Arnold's Army, Nicklaus's Navy, and Lema's Legions, the new champion got perhaps his biggest laugh when, as he was commenting on how much the cheering of the crowds had helped him all day long, he interrupted himself to say, "For years, all I ever heard was Venturi's Vultures." Perhaps he had said this before, but if he had no one was listening.

This selection is also taken from Following Through, *1985.*

JOHNNY MILLER, 1973 U.S. OPEN

Robert Sommers

The Best Round Ever?

Nicklaus had now won thirteen of the major tournaments, the same number but not the same events as Bobby Jones had won. It is difficult for men with the driving ambition and enormous egos necessary to reach apogee in any field to have heroes, but if Nicklaus had one, it was Jones. Jack had grown up in Columbus, Ohio. His father, Charles Nicklaus, was the owner of several pharmacies and held a membership in the Scioto Country Club, where Jones had won the 1926 Open. When Jack was a young boy, his father had told him stories of Jones. Indeed, Jones was a hero to the entire club, and so it was only natural for young Jack to set him up as an idol.

JOHNNY MILLER

When he retired after winning the original Grand Slam, Jones had won thirteen national championships—five U.S. Amateurs, one British Amateur, three British Opens, and four U.S. Opens. By the beginning of 1973, Nicklaus had won two U.S. Amateurs, four Masters Tournaments, two British Opens, two PGA Championships, and three U.S. Opens. He had not won the British Amateur.

At what point an idol becomes a rival is difficult to say. Indeed, it is not altogether certain that Nicklaus ever looked on Jones as anything other than a hero, but nevertheless Jack was driven to surpass Bobby's record, and by June of 1973 hardly anyone doubted he would.

The key goal was that fourth Open. Twenty years had passed since Hogan had won his fourth in 1953, and eleven years had gone by since Jack had won his first in 1962. Hogan had won his last and Nicklaus his first at Oakmont, and now the Open was back to that homely old course in the rolling hills of western Pennsylvania.

Oakmont was seventy years old by then, but it was expected to be just as tough as ever. It was twenty-seven yards longer than it had been in 1962, its fairways were still narrow, it was well bunkered—perhaps even excessively bunkered (thirty-three new ones had been added, bringing the total to 187)—and its greens were still the fastest in American golf, cut at three thirty-seconds of an inch for everyday play and even shorter for the Open. To emphasize driving accuracy, the USGA set fairway widths to an average of thirty-five yards—some short holes were narrower, some long holes were wider—but Oakmont members must have a masochistic streak in them, because the USGA ordained that two fairways had to be widened; they were too narrow for the Open field.

Oakmont made one other change, revising the 17th, which had always been its weakest hole. Hogan had driven the green in the last round in 1953 and birdied, and Palmer had driven it in the third round in 1962 and eagled. A new tee was built back in a wooded hollow behind and to the left of the old tee, the fairway was shifted to the right, and instead of 292 yards, it played now at 322 yards, with a big, sweeping right-to-left curve that brought into play the bunkers that framed the elevated green. The approach now had to carry those bunkers and hit and hold a shallow green. The 17th was much more satisfactory than it had been; no one could drive it now. But someone did.

Anticipation was at an unusually high pitch as the championship approached, the feeling more feverish than it had been in years. The reasons were varied. In addition to the game's having become a more popular spectator sport to begin with, Nicklaus was going for his fourth Open, his fourteenth major championship, and Palmer was still able to generate excitement, especially so close to home. This had been the scene of the confrontation of 1962, when Nicklaus had beaten Palmer, and Pennsylvania golf fans wanted revenge.

The weather for the first round was ideal for golf. The air was warm and light, and a little breeze blew from the west, helping the tee shots on the 17th. When he had finished sixteen holes, Nicklaus was two over par and unhappy, and seeing a chance to make up the strokes he had lost, he went for the 17th green. Drawing back his driver in his usual high arc, Jack swung with a combination of sheer power and perfect timing. The ball soared off in a high parabola, came down twenty yards short of the green, took one big bounce over the bunkers, and rolled ten feet from the cup. He holed the putt for an eagle 2 and finished the day at 71, four strokes behind Gary Player, who shocked the gallery by shaving four strokes from a sturdy par of 71 and shooting 67.

For Player to be at the front of the field was somewhat surprising, because he had been hospitalized for twelve days in February for surgery on his bladder, and had played in only three tournaments in five months. His 67 was a remarkable score, for Oakmont had been its usual difficult self, yielding birdies grudgingly. Player was enjoying a three-stroke lead over Lee Trevino, Jim Colbert, and Raymond Floyd, the only other men under par. Only six others matched par, and some of the scores were startling. Billy Casper shot 79, Bruce Devlin 76, Dow Finsterwald, Doug Ford and Bob Murphy, 77, Tony Jacklin 75, and Orville Moody 78. It looked as if this would be another trying week.

Then something happened overnight, and Oakmont was a different course on Friday. The greens had become soft, and the players were firing at the flagsticks without fear. The golf course was defenseless; it had never seen a day like this. Early in the day Gene Borek, a club professional from Long Island who was in the field as an alternate, shot 65 and broke the course record. Altogether nineteen men broke par. Brian Allin shot 67, Colbert 68, and nine others had 69, including Vinny Giles, the National Amateur champion, who had a great finish. Against a par of 4-3-4-4 he shot 2-3-3-3, holing a full 6-iron on the 15th, barely missing a birdie on the 16th, and holing short birdie putts on the 17th and 18th.

The sprinkling system was blamed. Unlike those at Pebble Beach and Merion, Oakmont's greens are large, and to be at their best, they must be firm and fast. Simply hitting them shouldn't be enough; you should be forced to hit the right spot. Reaching those spots is difficult if the greens are firm, but Pittsburgh had had a rainy spring, and on the Tuesday night before the championship began, Oakmont was hit by a thunderstorm. The weather had been clear and dry since then, and the course was becoming fast, just as it should be. When he shot his 67, Player said that by Sunday everybody would know just how good a round that was. Both P. J. Boatwright, the man most responsible for running the Open, and Harry Easterly, then the chairman of the championship committee, were satisfied the greens had the proper pace, and after a conversation with Lou Scalzo, the club's greenkeeper, they agreed to sprinkle for only five minutes overnight. Exactly what happened was never clear, but most likely someone made a mistake and allowed the sprinklers to run longer than they should have. Oakmont was never right again.

In the easier conditions, Player went around in 70, and while he clung to his lead, he was only a stroke ahead of Colbert, with 137 to 138. It was evident by now that Player's game was not as steady as his scores implied. With only twenty-nine putts for the round, he should have done better than 70, but five times he had to one-putt to save pars. Because he had been away from the game for so long, he did not have his usual competitive edge.

Nicklaus was hardly playing any better, but he was sharper competitively, and he could score. He birdied three of the last six holes, shot 69, and climbed to within three strokes of Player with 140. Palmer stood two strokes farther back after a second 71, but he was erratic. Every time he birdied, he threw the stroke away with a bogey. In thirty-six holes, he had had eight birdies, eight bogeys, and twenty pars.

Already saturated, Oakmont was hit by another storm early Saturday morning. Rain began falling heavily at about 5:30, stopped briefly three hours later, but began in earnest once again at about 9:30. It stopped in time for the first starting time at 10:20, but then fell heavily off and on throughout the day, occasionally interrupting play. While the greens had been soft on Friday, they were like mush on Saturday. Where the ball hit, it stopped. The course was playing easier than it ever had, but Player's game collapsed, and he shot 77. Six men broke 70, and when the round ended, four shared the lead at 210, another had 211, and three others had 212. Eight men were bunched within two strokes.

Jerry Heard was one of those at 210, after shooting 66, the low round of the day. A strapping six-footer who had dropped out of college to join the pro Tour in 1969, Heard said hitting irons to the greens was like throwing darts. He was tied with John Schlee, a lean, sandy-haired veteran with a flat, unattractive swing, fifty-three-year-old Julius Boros, and Palmer.

With so many bunched so close, and with Palmer among the leaders, a dramatic climax was shaping up for Sunday's final round, but some spectators who flooded through the gates came only to see Arnold. They had only a vague acquaintance with golf. To wit:

One man ran up to another and asked, "Where's the next par?"

Another wondered, "Do they change the pins for every group coming through?"

Still another looked at Arnold with green envy. Watching how the female spectators reacted as Palmer strode by, he turned to his companion and said, "Can you imagine being Arnold Palmer and single?"

Sunday was an uncomfortable day. Clouds hung low and the humidity pressed down, and because the overcast blocked the sun, the greens remained soft and receptive, raising the probability of low scoring. Nevertheless, no one was prepared for what happened.

Johnny Miller, a lanky, blond Californian who hit wonderfully straight and crisp irons and who had won two tournaments since dropping out of Brigham Young University to join the Tour in 1969, left the 1st tee an hour before the leaders. When he had left his motel that morning, he had told his wife to pack and be ready for a quick exit from Pittsburgh; after shooting an untidy 76 on Saturday, Miller had 216 for fifty-four holes and stood six strokes behind the leaders. To reach the top, he would have to pass twelve men; clearly, he was going nowhere.

Miller began the last round by playing a straight drive down the middle and then drilling one of his pretty, precise irons—a 5-iron here—five feet from the cup and holing the putt for a birdie.

"That's not too bad," he told himself. On to the 2nd.

After another straight drive, Miller almost holed his 9-iron; the ball sat down six inches from the cup for another birdie. On the 3rd he looked out at the Church Pew bunkers and smacked another long, straight drive and a 5-iron twenty-five feet past the hole. The putt fell; three under.

The fairway of the 4th, a 549-yard par 5, swings in a long crescent through a narrow opening past the Church Pews on the left and a grouping of five other bunkers on the right, through coarse and heavy rough to another slick and undulating green set at an angle to the approach. After another fine drive, Miller tried to reach the green with his second, but his 3-wood drifted into a greenside bunker on the right. He almost holed his recovery and had his fourth straight birdie. He had begun the day three over par and now he was one under for fifty-eight holes. For the first time it occurred to him that he could win.

No one was paying attention to Miller yet though, because at about this time the leaders were going off the 1st tee. Schlee was paired with Palmer, playing ahead of Boros and Heard, who were the last two men off. After Saturday's round, Schlee had tried to explain why he was playing so well. A disciple of astrology, he said, "My horoscope is just outstanding. Mars is in conjunction with my natal moon." Something must have tilted overnight, because he pushed his drive out of bounds and made 6 on the 1st hole. He would be back, though.

With so many players grouped so tightly, and almost all of them playing so well, it was impossible to tell what was happening through the first nine holes. Nicklaus set off a roar when he birdied the 2nd, but then so did Colbert, Trevino,

Bob Charles, and Tom Weiskopf. From then on through the end of the first nine, the situation changed quickly and repeatedly. Caught up in the frenzy, spectators dashed back and forth as one man after another went ahead, then fell back. Three men held the lead at one time or another—Heard after he birdied the 2nd, Palmer after a birdie on the 4th, then Boros after birdies on the 4th and 6th. As soon as they grabbed the lead, they lost it. After nine holes, Boros, Palmer, and Weiskopf shared the lead at four under par, and Trevino, Schlee, and Heard were three under.

Miller, meantime, had cooled off. After reeling off routine pars on the 5th, 6th, and 7th, he three-putted the 8th from thirty feet. Three under for the day now, he was four strokes behind the leaders, but he could pick up one with a birdie on the 9th, a short, uphill par 5. A drive, then a 2-iron, and he was on the green, but forty feet from the cup. A good lag putt put him close, and he holed the short second putt for the birdie. Out in 32 and four under par for the round, one under for sixty-three holes. Now he was closer, but a quick glance at the scoreboard showed him how tight the race had become. No one was folding; he needed more birdies.

A drive and 5-iron to twenty feet on the 10th. No birdie there. Then a break on the 11th. His wedge from the crest of the hill stopped fourteen feet away, and the putt fell. Five under for the day, two under for the distance. Closing in. Now for the 12th, 603 yards winding through wiry rough and deep bunkers. A drive into the rough, his first off-line drive of the day. No chance to do anything with this shot; just play it out to safety. A 7-iron to the fairway, then a marvelous 4-iron to fifteen feet. The putt dropped. Six under for the day, three under for the distance. Almost there.

Most of the gallery was still across the Pennsylvania Turnpike following Palmer, Boros, Nicklaus, and the others, but as word of Miller's hot streak spread, they raced for the footbridge that spans the Turnpike, clogging the approaches and cramming their way through. Risking serious injury, some fans climbed onto the foot-wide railing and crawled across on hands and knees while cars and trucks whizzed past below at mile-a-minute speeds. Others slipped off the course and fought their way through heavy traffic inching along a road that borders the club, then cut back onto the Oakmont grounds.

Miller kept up the pace. A 4-iron to five feet on the 13th and another putt dropped. Seven under for the day, four under for the distance. He'd caught up, and now only Palmer was tied with him. Another birdie chance on the 14th from twelve feet, but the ball stopped an inch from falling. Now for the 15th, one of the strongest holes in American golf, a 453-yard par 4 with a narrow fairway only thirty-four yards wide, bordered on the left by a smaller version of the Church Pews and on the right by a mammoth bunker that begins twenty yards ahead of the green and runs almost to the back edge. Putting something extra into the shot, Miller drove his ball 280 yards. Now a 4-iron. The ball hit the green, hopped once, and skidded ten feet away. Miller rolled the ball into the center of the hole. Eight under par for the round and finally into the lead at five under par for sixty-nine holes. Only three holes left.

Palmer, meanwhile, was coming up the 11th not aware of Miller's surge. He was four under par then, and after a good tee shot he played a lovely pitch just under four feet to the right of the hole. It seemed just like old times. If he kept playing as he was, he would surely win and have that second Open he had tried so hard for all those years. He was forty-three years old then, and he would probably have no more opportunities; he had to take advantage of this one. When he made this putt, he would be five under par, and that should be good enough.

Arnold was about to suffer three shocks that upset him so badly he never recovered.

First, he missed the putt and remained four under par. It hurt, but he believed he was still leading by a stroke over Schlee, Weiskopf, and Boros. Still confident, he strode over to the 12th tee and played what he thought was a perfect drive, shading the left side where the ground slants to the right and will kick the ball to center-fairway. He was so confident he had played the shot perfectly, he hitched his pants, and with an assured, tight-lipped smile, he turned away and didn't watch the ball land.

Then, as he and Schlee left the tee, Arnold glanced at a scoreboard. Squinting through the branches of a tree, Palmer made out a red 5 down on the bottom of the board indicating that someone was five under par and a stroke ahead of him. He couldn't quite make out the name.

Palmer was stunned. His confident grin faded and, bewildered, he asked Schlee, "Who's five under?"

"Miller," Schlee answered. "Didn't you know?" Shock number two.

Then, as he and Schlee approached the landing area, they saw only one ball in the fairway. Assuming it was his, Arnold strode up to it, but when he looked down, he saw it was Schlee's. Instead of bouncing right, Palmer's ball had jumped left into heavy rough. Shock number three. He bogeyed the 12th, then followed with two more bogeys on the 13th and 14th. There would be no second Open.

Now it was only a matter of Miller's holding on. A 3-wood to forty feet on the 16th and two putts for a par 3; a 1-iron and a wedge to ten feet on the 17th and another par; then a huge drive on the 18th, a 7-iron to twenty feet, and two more putts for his final par. Out in 32, back in 31. A 63, the lowest round ever shot in the Open.

Miller finished with 279, four strokes better than Hogan had shot in 1953 and than Nicklaus and Palmer had shot in 1962, and twenty strokes under Sam Parks's 299 of 1935.

But it wasn't over yet; two men could still catch him.

Schlee had rallied after his 6 on the 1st hole, and now he could tie Miller with a birdie on the 18th. His second shot rolled over the green into clumpy rough about fifty feet from the hole. He would have to chip. The crowd hushed and Miller stood and watched as Schlee set himself. He played a courageous shot, gauging the distance just right, but he pulled the ball a trifle left of the hole and made 4.

Miller relaxed. Only Weiskopf was left, and he would have to hole his second shot on the 18th to tie. He didn't, and Miller was the champion. Schlee finished second, one stroke behind at 280, and Weiskopf was third at 281. Palmer, Trevino and Nicklaus all shot 282, and Boros and Heard finished with 283, tied with Lanny Wadkins.

Miller had played a phenomenal round. He had hit every green and had missed only one fairway on the driving holes. His irons were inspiring. He had hit five shots inside six feet (two of them inside one foot), two more to ten feet, and three others to fifteen feet or less. He had birdied nine holes and had bogeyed only the 8th, where he had three-putted. His 63 had broken the record set first by Lee Mackey at Merion in 1950, then matched by Tommy Jacobs at Congressional in 1964, and by Rives McBee at Olympic in 1966.

As soon as Miller posted his score, a natural question arose: Was it the greatest round ever played in the Open? Did it rank with the 65 Arnold Palmer shot at Cherry Hills in 1960, the round that carried him to the championship from seven strokes behind, or with Ben Hogan's closing 67 at Oakland Hills in 1951?

No, it didn't. While it was an extraordinary score, it was done over a course softened by rain. Miller's shots required nowhere near the control of Palmer's and Hogan's, because they played their rounds over fast and firm courses. For them to hold those hard greens, Palmer and Hogan had to play to certain spots on the greens and apply fierce backspin to stop the ball. Miller didn't have to do that: Oakmont's greens were so soft and mushy, any kind of shot would hold.

Nevertheless, Miller had played the course as he found it, and he had played it better than anyone else. As for controlling his emotions, while it is true he had no thoughts of winning when he had begun in the morning, he had realized he had a chance after he birdied the first four holes, and he had birdied five more after that. Furthermore, a 63 on no matter what kind of course is something special, and even though Oakmont was playing easier in 1973 than it had ever played, it was still among the more challenging tests in American golf.

Miller's 63 wasn't the best ever, but it was close.

Robert Sommers is the author of Golf Anecdotes *and* The U.S. Open: Golf's Ultimate Challenge *from which this excerpt is taken.*

JACK NICKLAUS

THE ROUND
JACK NICKLAUS
FORGOT (1978)

Red Smith

1978

J ack Nicklaus's golf is better than his memory. When he came charging home in the Inverray Classic last weekend, picking up four strokes on Grier Jones, three on Jerry Pate and Andy Bean, and two on Hale Irwin with five birdies on the last five holes, he was asked whether he had ever put on such a finish before. "I can't imagine any other time," he said. "It was the most remarkable thing I've ever seen in my life," said Lee Trevino, comparing it with Reggie Jackson's three home runs in the last World Series game and Leon Spinks' victory over Muhammad Ali. Well, it was remarkable but it wasn't unprecedented.

Fifteen years ago, Nicklaus and Arnold Palmer represented the United States in the World Cup competition at Saint-Nom-la-Bretèche near Versailles in France. If Jack has forgotten his performance there, perhaps he wanted to forget it. Maybe he deliberately put it out of his mind as too outrageously theatrical to bear remembering.

The things he did on the very first hole were downright scandalous. The hole was a legitimate par 5 for club members but a trifle short for a pro with Jack's power, measuring somewhere between 450 and 500 yards. In his four rounds, Jack played it eagle, eagle, eagle, birdie, and that was just for openers.

Bretèche may have been a trifle shorter than Inverray's 7,127 yards, but this was no exhibition on a pitch-and-putt course, and the opposition was at least as distinguished as the field Nicklaus encountered last week. The World Cup, now twenty-five years old, is a movable feast that leaps from continent to continent, usually playing national capitals, matching two-man teams from virtually every land where the game is known. Though it hasn't the prestige of the United States or British Open, it is probably the closest thing there is to a world championship.

In 1963, Saint-Nom-la-Bretèche was a comparatively new course built on land that had been the royal farm when Louis XIV was top banana. The clubhouse, once the royal cow barn, was a splendid building of ivy-covered stone set in a terraced stableyard ablaze with roses, snapdragon, chrysanthemum and pansies.

The galleries had a touch of quality seldom associated with, say, Maple Moor in Westchester County. Among those who followed the play were two former kings and one former Vice President—Leopold of Belgium, the Duke of Windsor and Richard M. Nixon.

Before play started, Prince Michel de Bourbon-Parme, the club president, dispatched ten dozen fresh eggs to a nearby convent. This, he explained, was an ancient custom in the Ile de France. Anyone planning an outdoor binge like a wedding or garden party sent eggs to the poor and this assured him of good weather. The standard fee was one dozen eggs, but the Prince had laid it on to guarantee a week of sunshine.

Morning of the opening round found the Prince glowering through a clammy fog. "So," he said, "I am sending to the sisters to get back my eggs."

Soggy turf made the course play long for little guys, but not for Nicklaus. His second shot on the opening hole was twenty feet from the pin, and he ran down the putt for his first eagle 3. After that he had five birdies and three bogeys for a 67. Palmer's 69 gave the pair a tie for first place with Al Balding and Stan Leonard of Canada.

Prince Michel changed his mind about reclaiming the eggs, but the weather didn't relent. Day by day the fog thickened, until the green hills and yellow bunkers were all but blotted out. Realizing that if a hitter like Nicklaus tried to fire a tee shot into that soup the ball would never be seen again, officials postponed the final round for twenty-four hours.

It didn't help much. Next day a gray soufflé garnished the fairways. The climate dripped sullenly from the trees. Windsor and Leopold showed up as they had for each earlier round, but the weather reduced the gallery to a minimum. Reluctantly, the committee decided to cut the final round to nine holes. At this point Nicklaus and Palmer were tied with Spain's Ramon Sota and Sebastian Miguel for the team trophy, with Nicklaus and Gary Player all square in individual competition.

Automobiles were driven out past the first green, where they made a U-turn and parked with headlights on. From the tee, lights were blurred but visible, giving the players a target. For the first time in four rounds, Nicklaus needed four shots to get down. Then he got serious.

With that birdie for a start, he played the next five holes as follows: 3-3-3-3-3. When he walked toward the seventh tee, a spectator asked: "What are you going to do for an encore?"

"Try to finish," Jack said.

On the first six holes he had taken 19 shots. On the last three he took 13 for a 32. It won.

Red Smith was considered not just a great sportswriter but a great writer who happened to write about sports. This article was written in 1978.

TOM WATSON, 1982 U.S. OPEN

Thomas Boswell

The Chip

Pebble Beach, California, June 20, 1982—

Fifteen years ago, when he was just a teenager and Jack Nicklaus was already established as the king of golf, Tom Watson would find a way, on Sunday mornings, to be the first dew-sweeping player on the Pebble Beach Golf Links.

"I'd drive down here from Stanford [University] and tee it up at seven A.M., when I'd have the whole course to myself," said Watson this evening. "Honestly, I did fantasize about coming down the stretch head to head with Jack Nicklaus in the U.S. Open.

TOM WATSON

"Then I'd get to the last couple of holes and say, 'You've gotta play these one under par to win the Open,'. Of course, I'd always play 'em two over. And I'd say, 'You have a long way to go, kid.'"

Tom Watson has had to come a long, slow, arduous way. But today, all his fantasies, plus one piece of magic so outlandish that even a boy playing at sunrise would never dream it, became reality. And history.

With one shot that will live in the retelling as long as golf is played, Watson wiped away—like a Pacific fog along the cliffs evaporating with the morning sun—the last blemish on his great and growing record.

Years from now, it will probably be forgotten that Watson won this 82nd U.S. Open by two shots over Nicklaus in a breath-stopping back-nine duel. In time, the details of this misty Monterey evening may fade—even the trenchant fact that, with Nicklaus and his 69 (284 total) already in the clubhouse, Watson finished birdie-birdie on the 71st and 72nd holes to slash his way out of a tie with the fabled Golden Bear.

In 19th-hole lore, only a few will recall that Watson's pilgrimage to his first Open title was carved out with a week of creditable work (72-72-68-70) for a six-under-par total of 282. To be sure, no one will recall that Bill Rogers (74), Bobby Clampett (70) and Dan Pohl (70) tied for third at 286.

In the end, only one moment—one shot that epitomizes both Watson and his game—will last. Already Watson calls it "the shot . . . the greatest shot of my life, the most meaningful."

It's that one swing, and no other, that prompted Nicklaus to grab Watson in a fraternal bear hug as he stepped off the final green and tell him, "You son of a . . . you're something else. I'm really proud of you."

Naturally, Watson remembers the embrace a bit differently: "Jack said, 'I'm gonna beat you, you little SOB, if it takes me the rest of my life.'"

So, for the moment, we will forget how Watson began the day tied for the lead with Rogers. We will pass over the jubilation that swept this seaside links as the dormant Nicklaus birdied five straight holes on the front nine—the 3rd through the 7th—to forge, momentarily, into a one-shot lead.

We will negligently dash past the details of how two bogeys by Nicklaus—one perhaps abetted by a former U.S. President—plus a cross-country birdie by Watson, pushed the thirty-two-year-old redhead back into the lead by two shots. And, finally, we will gloss over Nicklaus's classy birdie at the 15th and Watson's wild drive and bogey at the 16th that deadlocked the pair for the lead one final time.

The scene thus set, we must return to the one moment from this Open that will outlast and, unfortunately, diminish all others. Outlined against the blue-gray sky of Carmel Bay, Watson stands locked in ankle-deep rough beside the 17th green. In trying for a daring birdie—hitting a two-iron into the breeze at the 209-yard par-3, Watson has, instead, put himself in just the predicament for which Jack Neville built this course in 1919.

No shot in golf is a better test of nerves, experience and touch than the "grass explosion" from high, unforgiving U.S. Open rough to a pin on a glass-slick green that is only 18 feet away.

Watching on TV, Nicklaus, who was going for a record fifth Open title and twentieth major, says he thought, "There's no way in the world he can get up-and-down from there [for par]. Even if he has a good lie, you couldn't drop the ball straight down out of your hand on that green and keep it from going less than ten feet past the pin. I figured: Now he's going to have to birdie the last hole just to tie me and get into a playoff [on Monday]."

Watson's opinion was different. "I'm not trying to get this close," he recalled telling his caddie. "I'm going to make it."

Why shouldn't he have thought so? Perhaps no man since Arnold Palmer in his prime has so consistently willed the ball into the hole from ludicrously improper places. On the 10th, Watson was on a cliffside amidst wildflowers; he hacked to the fringe 24 feet away and sank his Texas-wedge shot to save par. On the 11th, he sank a 22-footer from the fringe for a birdie. And at the 14th, he was in the frog hair again, and holed out from 35 feet. As Nicklaus put it: "Yes, yes, I heard about all those shots. Just another tap-in for Tom."

With this preternatural confidence, which is his trademark, Watson stepped into the weeds by the 17th quickly and, opening the face of his sand wedge, "sliced across the ball and slid the edge of the club under it. It was a good lie, with the ball hanging in the middle of the grass. If it had been down, I'd have had no shot. . . .

"As soon as it landed on the green, I knew it was in," said Watson, whose whole face was alive with hunger as the ball trickled and broke—a full foot and a half from left to right.

"When it went in the hole, I about jumped in the Pacific Ocean," said Watson with a laugh. He ran at least twenty yards around the edge of the green, his putter over his head in victory and his feet carrying him he knew not where. Then, commanding himself, Watson spun and pointed at his caddie and yelled, "Told ya!"

"He was chokin', chokin' bad," Watson said with a grin. "He couldn't utter anything."

Neither could Nicklaus. "When he makes that, the golf tournament's history. . . . I've had it happen before, but I didn't think it was going to happen again. But it did. . . . How would I evaluate that shot? One of the worst that ever happened to me. Right up there with [Lee] Trevino's [chip-in] at Muirfield [on the 71st hole of the '72 British Open]."

An almost certain bogey that probably would have lost his Open and branded Watson a gagger had been turned, in a twinkling, into one of the most gloriously improbable Open-winning birdies in history.

Had Watson merely parred the 17th, he would have had to birdie the 18th to win. And nobody has ever birdied the 72nd hole of the Open to win. As it was, Watson's downhill 18-foot birdie on the last hole was a wonderful crescendo for a day full of tremulously rolling drums. But had Watson needed to make it to win, it might have been a tougher proposition.

Watson's playing partner, Rogers, said of that soft shot into history, "He couldn't have hit a better shot if he'd dropped down a hundred balls."

"Try about a thousand," said Nicklaus drolly.

Told of Nicklaus's oddsmaking, Watson—as superb a greenside magician as Nicklaus has always been bear-pawed—said, "Let's go out and do it. I might make some money."

Watson faced up to every sort of Open pressure today. "I was on pins and needles all day."

Watson woke up nervous, then calmed himself by reading two newspapers "front to back. Ask me anything about the earthquake in El Salvador or the budget problems." His swing was loosey-goosey all day—he missed only one fairway, but his putting was nervous and cold on the front nine, especially when he missed a two-foot birdie putt at the 7th.

Perhaps Watson was unhinged by all those bear tracks he had to walk through. As he trudged through the 3rd through the 7th, all he heard was buzzing talk about how Nicklaus, after a shoddy bogey-par start, had been knocking down flags for five consecutive holes. By the time Nicklaus had made two-foot tap-ins for birdie at the 5th and 6th, he was tied for the lead. And when he sank a 12-foot curler at the gorgeous 7th to take the lead, his caddie—son Jack Jr.—jumped nearly two feet in the air and began applauding.

Nicklaus misclubbed himself at the over-a-gorge 8th and was lucky to make bogey from a hanging lie on the edge of a precipice. That, however, won't be the bogey that haunts him. At the 11th, tied for the lead, he had a flat, slightly downhill 18-foot birdie putt that he slid four feet past and missed coming back. What could have accounted for his only mental lapse of the day?

No one will ever know for sure, but lovers of anecdote might enjoy the fact that former President Gerald Ford, a notorious three-putter, walked down from a course-side house and stood conspicuously by the 11th green as Nicklaus three-putted. Ford then came forward to shake Nicklaus's hand and exchange pleasantries at the 12th tee—an intrusion into serious work that no normal citizen would, presumably, have dared to attempt. Call it the Presidential Bogey or Jerry's Whammy.

In the gathering dusk around America's most lustrously atmospheric links, Watson was aglow with pride and vindication. Asked, teasingly, "Why can't you win the PGA?" he said, "Up till now, it's been: Why couldn't Sam Snead and I win the Open? Now it'll be: Why can't Arnold Palmer and I win the PGA? Well, I'll stay here all night and talk about it."

Time and again, Watson had to return, as he will have the pleasure of returning for the rest of his life, to the Impossible Shot.

"I had no alternative," Watson said finally, with his best freckled, gap-toothed smile. "For you, it's impossible."

But not for this country's overdue and deserving U.S. Open champion.

Thomas Boswell is a sports columnist for The Washington Post *and author of such books as* The Heart of the Order *and* Strokes of Genius. *This piece is from* Game Day, *1990.*

JACK NICKLAUS

JACK NICKLAUS, 1986 MASTERS

Wilfred Sheed

The Old Man and the Tee

There are certain things you never get to see in life because there aren't enough cameras to go around. For instance, the look on a painter's face when he stares at his latest baby and decides that it's finally finished—one more stroke and he could have blown it; or the novelist coming down the home-stretch; or the scientist contemplating his slide and realizing that that unappetizing blob of muck on it spells either glory or twenty years down the tube.

We did, however, get to see Jack Nicklaus play the last four holes at the Masters Tournament this spring (spring for us, that is, autumn for him—non-golf fanciers should be apprised that this was the second oldest man ever to win a major tournament, coming from four strokes down with only four holes to play and passing a menacing herd of young tigers on his way).

To go with his sizzling performance, Nicklaus happened to be wearing the most expressive face I've ever seen on an athlete—because in his own special world he *was* an artist working on a masterpiece that one extra stroke would literally ruin, a scientist with a pack of rivals baying at his heels as he pondered each putt. But above all, he was playing a sport that allows one to show, indeed almost forbids one not to show, one's thoughts.

Consider the alternatives. Football players, bless them, never have to show their faces at all. Baseball hitters' mouths, as photographed, open foolishly at the moment of contact, while pitchers do their best to look like poker players or shell-game operators, which in a sense they are. In track, sprinters' faces tend to burst at the seams, while long-distance guys run as if they were down to their last tank: one animate expression might dislodge something vital in there.

Tennis players have the time to look interesting, but they waste great gobs of it glaring at the linesmen or the umpire or at anything that moves—still, they have their moments. Basketball players seesaw interminably between goofy elation and grim determination all the live night long. With hockey players, who can tell? A man without teeth looks like the Mona Lisa at the best of times, bomb damage at the worst. Jockeys probably look fascinating, but who has time to notice? Golfers for their part do not exactly whiz by: for days they move like snails under glass, until we know every last twitch, with time left over to memorize their wardrobe and decipher its meanings.

However, there was more to Nicklaus' face that day than simple visibility. He is a disciplined man, and there had to be a lot in there for so much to come out. The first item in the making of the Face was simply that of his age; at forty-six, Nicklaus is at least old enough to *have* a face, as they say in Ireland. But he is also much too old to win a major golf tournament, and this thought must have followed him around the course like a playground pest jumping on his back and trying to pinion his arms, all the while jabbering, "You can't do it because it can't be done, *you can't do . . .*" Scat, said Nicklaus' face. Get that bum out of here. But not until the Face lit up, like Broadway, on the eighteenth green, could we be sure the bum had left.

Then there was the occasion. The Masters is far and away our classiest tournament—the one the Duchess of Kent would attend if we had a Duchess of Kent. And since Nicklaus' appearances anywhere at this point are on the order of royal visits in themselves, the combination is enough to make even a spectator's knees tremble. The gale-force waves of adulation that crash over the guest of honor on such occasions must make it all the victim can do just to smile and wave weakly like the queen. So imagine her royal self being handed a set of clubs and commanded to play right through the crowd, all the way to the coronation, pitching her ball up the steps and into a little tin cup, before she can claim her crown.

That is more or less what King Jack had to do to get his green jacket, and he admitted that he had to fight tears several times as he strode down those last ringing fairways. Wouldn't it be pleasanter just to relax and enjoy this? It's such a lovely course. . . . No, said the Face.

A third, more mundane factor in the making of Nicklaus' Face was the simple fact that Nicklaus can't see as well as he used to and no longer has the pleasure of watching those intergalactic drives of his return to Earth. For the Masters, therefore, his son had to double as caddy and long-range seeing-eye dog, which added for this reporter a curiously Biblical touch to the proceedings. But besides all that, myopia in itself can produce a lightly strained appearance that, as I learned back in school, can pass for thinking if you play it right.

Of course, the fourth factor or facet, in the Face was that Nicklaus wasn't "playing it" at all. By the fifteenth hole, he probably wasn't even aware that he *had* a face, and he certainly didn't give a damn what it looked like. In fact, if the Devil had popped the question, I dare say old Jack would have willingly put on a fright wig and a bright-red nose in exchange for just one more twenty-five-footer.

Or at least *I* would have. I guess it hardly needs pointing out that all the above was going on in my mind, not his, and that watching a game can be even more nerve-racking than playing one, as I learned from a priest friend who bit clear through his umbrella handle while watching a cricket match. What Nicklaus actually said when this seeming agony in Bobby Jones' garden was over was that he had felt "comfortable" (comfortable!) over the twenty-five-footers and that he hadn't had so much fun in six years.

Well, a champion's idea of fun may not be everybody's. Amounts of tension that would send a normal man screaming into the woods act on him like a tonic, or a wake-up call. Athletes have been known to complain of not feeling enough of it ("man, I was flat out there"). Basketball's super-cool Bill Russell—and doubtless many others less cool—used routinely to throw up before outings, so that it became almost part of his regimen. John McEnroe favors a level of constant embarrassment to light his phlegm, while Muhammad Ali's weigh-in tantrums used to send his blood pressure into the stratosphere.

But a golfer has no need of such paltry devices. All he has to do is think about putting. The great Sam Snead for one could never resign himself to the idea that this dwarfish stroke, the putt, should count every bit as much as a booming three-hundred-yard drive, and he actually wanted putting declared a separate sport.

It certainly *looks* different. Every other stroke, I am assured, can be played with the same basic swing, variously adjusted — that is, until one approaches the pressure pit, or green, at which point the whole exercise changes its nature from a robust, swinging affair to a pinched little game of skill suitable for saloons. The lords of the fairway are suddenly called upon to hunch over like bank clerks and not move a muscle. The result is almost an anti-swing, a total negation of everything they've been doing. The shoulders remain still, the hips don't swivel, the wrists break not. From behind, the golfer appears to be doing nothing at all, but that's not quite so; what he's doing is growing an ulcer.

That low growl that hangs over the nation's golf courses at all times is mostly about putting. At least in the rough you can hack your way out and mutilate some of the course in revenge, while with water hazards you get to roll up your pants and have a nice paddle. But putting is like drinking tea with your pinkie raised, or more precisely, like threading a needle with a thread that bends at the last moment. (Tournament greens, by the way, are not to be compared with miniature gold; they are more, if you can stand another metaphor, like ice that tilts.)

Testimonials to the human toll exacted by this disgusting practice can be picked up anywhere the strange game is played. The incomparable Ben Hogan had to quit the game because of it. Although Hogan's nerves had won him the name of "Iceman," and although the rest of his game still glittered, he suddenly succumbed to something known as the yips, a degenerative ailment that freezes the hands in terror and renders them incapable of so much as lifting the club head back.

Out of sheer and unprecedented compassion, the unbending masters of gold bent just enough to let Snead use a club shaped like a T square during his later years, with which he could practically putt from between his legs like an aging croquet player (it didn't help). Gene Sarazen, the Grandma

Moses of the game, once suggested, but was *not* granted, a six-inch hole. And if the word of an outsider is of any help, Dick Groat, who played shortstop for the Pirates in the hair-raising seven-game World Series of 1960, said that he didn't know what pressure was until he stepped onto the eighteenth green in a pro-am tournament.

This is the stuff that Nicklaus feels "comfortable" with? Well, saints be praised. One falls back in awe as a champion so simply and casually defines what the word means. He didn't *look* comfortable, but that had nothing to do with it. He looked, among other things, eager, speculative, and about ready to cry. But inside he apparently felt the kind of joy that inhuman pressure brings only to heroes, and you didn't need to be a golf buff to have felt happy to share a species with such a man as the green jacket was finally slipped over his shoulders.

Wilfred Sheed has been nominated for three National Book Awards in fiction and for the National Book Critics' Circle Award in Criticism. His portrait of Jack Nicklaus, while not a "great comeback," gives us a fascinating look at the Golden Bear's face during the 1986 Masters.

FROM:
GOLDFINGER

Ian Fleming

They came up with the green. Goldfinger had pitched on and had a long putt for a four, but Bond's ball was only two inches away from the hole. Goldfinger picked up his ball and walked off the green. They halved the short sixteenth in good threes. Now there were the two long holes home. Fours would win them. Bond hit a fine drive down the centre. Goldfinger pushed his far out to the right into deep rough. Bond walked along trying not to be too jubilant, trying not to count his chickens. A win for him at this hole and he would only need a half at the eighteenth for the match. He prayed that Goldfinger's ball would be unplayable or, better still, lost.

SEAN CONNERY
AS JAMES BOND

Hawker had gone on ahead. He had already laid down his bag and was busily—far too busily to Bond's way of thinking—searching for Goldfinger's ball when they came up.

It was bad stuff—jungle country, deep thick luxuriant grass whose roots still held last night's dew. Unless they were very lucky, they couldn't hope to find the ball. After a few minutes' search Goldfinger and his caddie drifted away still wider to where the rough thinned out into isolated tufts. That's good, thought Bond. That wasn't anything like the line. Suddenly he trod on something. Hell and damnation. Should he stamp it in? He shrugged his shoulders, bent down and gently uncovered the ball so as not to improve the lie. Yes it was a Dunlop 65. 'Here you are,' he called grudgingly. 'Oh no, sorry. You play with a Number One, don't you?'

'Yes,' came back Goldfinger's voice impatiently.

'Well, this is a Number Seven.' Bond picked it up and walked over to Goldfinger.

Goldfinger gave the ball a cursory glance. He said, 'Not mine,' and went on poking among the tufts with the head of his driver.

It was a good ball, unmarked and almost new. Bond put it in his pocket and went back to his search. He glanced at his watch. The statutory five minutes was almost up. Another half-minute and by God he was going to claim the hole. Strict rules of golf, Goldfinger had stipulated. All right my friend, you shall have them!

Goldfinger was casting back towards Bond, diligently prodding and shuffling through the grass.

Bond said, 'Nearly time, I'm afraid.'

Goldfinger grunted. He started to say something when there came a cry from his caddie, 'Here you are, sir. Number One Dunlop.'

Bond followed Goldfinger over to where the caddie stood on a small plateau of higher ground. He was pointing down.

Bond bent and inspected the ball. Yes, an almost new Dunlop One and in an astonishingly good lie. It was miraculous—more than miraculous. Bond stared hard from Goldfinger to his caddie. 'Must have had the hell of a lucky kick,' he said mildly.

The caddie shrugged his shoulders. Goldfinger's eyes were calm, untroubled. 'So it would seem.' He turned to his caddie, 'I think we can get a spoon to that one, Foulks.'

Bond walked thoughtfully away and then turned to watch the shot. It was one of Goldfinger's best. It soared over a far shoulder of rough towards the green. Might just have caught the bunker on the right.

Bond walked on to where Hawker, a long blade of grass dangling from his wry lips, was standing on the fairway watching the shot finish. Bond smiled bitterly at him. He said in a controlled voice, 'Is my good friend in the bunker, or is the bastard on the green?'

'Green, sir,' said Hawker unemotionally.

Bond went up to his ball. Now things had got tough again. Once more he was fighting for a half after having a certain win in his pocket. He glanced toward the pin, gauging the distance. This was a tricky one. He said, 'Five or six?'

'The six should do it, sir. Nice firm shot,' Hawker handed him the club.

Now then, clear your mind. Keep it slow and deliberate. It's an easy shot. Just punch it so that it's got plenty of zip to get up the bank and on to the green. Stand still and head down. Click! The ball, hit with a slightly closed face, went off on just the medium trajectory Bond had wanted. It pitched below the bank. It was perfect! No, damn it. It had hit the bank with its second bounce, stopped dead, hesitated and then rolled back and down again. Hell's bells! Was it Hagen who had said, 'You drive for show, but you putt for dough'? Getting dead from below that bank was one of the most difficult putts on the course. Bond reached for his cigarettes and lit one, already preparing his mind for the next crucial shot to save the hole — so long as that bastard Goldfinger didn't hole his from thirty feet!

Hawker walked along by his side. Bond said, 'Miracle finding that ball.'

'It wasn't his ball, sir.' Hawker was stating a fact.

'What do you mean?' Bond's voice was tense.

'Money passed, sir. White, probably a fiver. Foulks must have dropped that ball down his trouser leg.'

'Hawker!' Bond stopped in his tracks. He looked round. Goldfinger and his caddie were fifty yards away, walking slowly towards the green. Bond said fiercely, 'Do you swear to that? How can you be sure?'

Hawker gave a half-ashamed, lop-sided grin. But there was a crafty belligerence in his eye. 'Because his ball was lying under my bag of clubs, sir.' When he saw Bond's open-mouthed expression he added apologetically, 'Sorry, sir. Had to do it after what he's been doing to you. Wouldn't have mentioned it, but I had to let you know he's fixed you again.'

Bond had to laugh. He said admiringly, 'Well, you *are* a card, Hawker. So you were going to win the match for me all on your own!' He added bitterly, 'But, by God, that man's the flaming limit. I've got to get him. I've simply got to. Now let's think!' They walked slowly on.

Bond's left hand was in his trousers pocket, absent-mindedly fingering the ball he had picked up in the rough. Suddenly the message went to his brain. Got it! He came close to Hawker. He glanced across at the others. Goldfinger had stopped. His back was to Bond and he was taking the putter out of his bag. Bond nudged Hawker. 'Here, take this.' He slipped the ball into the gnarled hand. Bond said softly, urgently, 'Be certain you take the flag. When you pick up the balls from the green, whichever way the hole has gone, give Goldfinger this one. Right?'

Hawker walked stolidly forward. His face was expressionless. 'Got it, sir,' he said in his normal voice. 'Will you take the putter for this one?'

'Yes.' Bond walked up to his ball. 'Give me a line, would you?'

Hawker walked up on to the green. He stood sideways to the line of the putt and then stalked round to behind the flag and crouched. He got up. 'Inch outside the right lip, sir. Firm putt. Flag, sir?'

'No. Leave it in, would you.'

Hawker stood away. Goldfinger was standing by his ball on the right of the green. His caddie had stopped at the bottom of the slope. Bond bent to the putt. Come on, Calamity Jane! This one has got to go dead or I'll put you across my knee. Stand still. Club head straight back on the line and follow through towards the hole. Give it a chance. Now! The ball, hit firmly in the middle of the club, had run up the bank and was on its way to the hole. But too hard, damn it! Hit the stick! Obediently the ball curved in, rapped the stick hard and bounced back three inches—dead as a doornail!

Bond let out a deep sigh and picked up his discarded cigarette. He looked over at Goldfinger. Now then, you bastard. Sweat that one out. And by God if you hole it! But Goldfinger couldn't afford to try. He stopped two feet short. 'All right, all right,' said Bond generously. 'All square and one to go.' It was vital that Hawker should pick up the balls. If he had made Goldfinger hole the short putt it would have been Goldfinger who would have picked the ball out of the hole. Anyway, Bond didn't want Goldfinger to miss that putt. That wasn't part of the plan.

Hawker bent down and picked up the balls. He rolled one towards Bond and handed the other to Goldfinger. They walked off the green, Goldfinger leading as usual. Bond noticed Hawker's hand go to his pocket. Now, so long as Goldfinger didn't notice anything on the tee!

But, with all square and one to go, you don't scrutinize your ball. Your motions are more or less automatic. You are think-ing of how to place your drive, of whether to go for the green with the second or play to the apron, of the strength of the wind—of the vital figure four that must somehow be achieved to win or at least to halve.

Considering that Bond could hardly wait for Goldfinger to follow him and hit, just once, that treacherous Dunlop Number Seven that looked so very like a Number One, Bond's own drive down the four hundred and fifty yard eighteenth was praiseworthy. If he wanted to, he could now reach the green— if he wanted to!

Now Goldfinger was on the tee. Now he had bent down. The ball was on the peg, its lying face turned up at him. But Goldfinger had straightened, had stood back, was taking his two deliberate practice swings. He stepped up to the ball, cautiously, deliberately. Stood over it, waggled, focusing the ball minutely. Surely he would see! Surely he would stop and bend down at the last minute to inspect the ball! Would the waggle never end? But now the club head was going back, coming down, the left knee bent correctly in towards the ball, the left arm straight as a ramrod. Crack! The ball sailed off, a beautiful drive, as good as Goldfinger had hit, straight down the fairway.

Bond's heart sang. Got you, you bastard! Got you! Blithely Bond stepped down from the tee and strolled off down the fair-way planning the next steps which could now be as eccentric, as fiendish as he wished. Goldfinger was beaten already—hoist with his own petard! Now to roast him, slowly, exquisitely.

Bond had no compunction. Goldfinger had cheated him twice and got away with it. But for his cheats at the Virgin and the seventeenth, not to mention his improved lie at the third and the various times he had tried to put Bond off, Goldfinger would have been beaten by now. If it needed one cheat by Bond to rectify the score-sheet that was only poetic justice. And beside, there was more to this than a game of golf. It was Bond's duty to win. By his reading of Goldfinger he *had* to win. If he was beaten, the score between the two men would have been equalized. If he won the match, as he now had, he would be two up on Goldfinger—an intolerable state of affairs, Bond guessed, to a man who saw himself as all powerful. This man Bond, Goldfinger would say to himself, *has* something. He has qualities I can use. He is a tough adventurer with plenty of tricks up his sleeve. This is the sort of man I need for—for what? Bond didn't know. Perhaps there would be nothing for him. Perhaps his reading of Goldfinger was wrong, but there was certainly no other way of creeping up on the man.

Goldfinger cautiously took out his spoon for the longish second over cross-bunkers to the narrow entrance to the green. He made one more practice swing than usual and then hit exactly the right, controlled shot up to the apron. A certain five, probably a four. Much good would it do him!

Bond, after a great show of taking pains, brought his hands down well ahead of the club and smothered his number three iron so that the topped ball barely scrambled over the cross-bunkers. He then wedged the ball on to the green twenty feet past the pin. He was where he wanted to be—enough of a threat to make Goldfinger savour the sweet smell of victory, enough to make Goldfinger really sweat to get his four.

And now Goldfinger really was sweating. There was a savage grin of concentration and greed as he bent to the long putt up the bank and down to the hole. Not too hard, not too soft. Bond could read every anxious thought that would be running through the man's mind. Goldfinger straightened up again, walked deliberately across the green to behind the flag to verify his line. He walked slowly back beside his line, brushing away—carefully, with the back of his hand—a wisp or two of grass, a speck of top-dressing. He bent again and made one or two practice swings and then stood to the putt, the veins standing out on his temples, the cleft of concentration deep between his eyes.

Goldfinger hit the putt and followed through on the line. It was a beautiful putt that stopped six inches past the pin. Now Goldfinger would be sure that unless Bond sank his difficult twenty-footer, the match was his!

Bond went through a long rigmarole of sizing up his putt. He took his time, letting the suspense gather like a thunder cloud round the long shadows on the livid, fateful green.

'Flag out, please. I'm going to sink this one.' Bond charged the words with a deadly certitude, while debating whether to miss the hole to the right or the left or leave it short. He bent to the putt and missed the hole well on the right.

'Missed it, by God!' Bond put bitterness and rage into his voice. He walked over to the hole and picked up the two balls, keeping them in full view.

Goldfinger came up. His face was glistening with triumph. 'Well, thanks for the game. Seems I was just too good for you after all.'

'You're a good nine handicap,' said Bond with just sufficient sourness. He glanced at the balls in his hand to pick out Goldfinger's and hand it to him. He gave a start of surprise. 'Hullo!' He looked sharply at Goldfinger. 'You play a Number One Dunlop, don't you?'

'Yes, of course.' A sixth sense of disaster wiped the triumph off Goldfinger's face. 'What is it? What's the matter?'

'Well,' said Bond apologetically, ''Fraid you've been playing with the wrong ball. Here's my Penfold Hearts and this is a Number Seven Dunlop.' He handed both balls to Goldfinger. Goldfinger tore them off his palm and examined them feverishly.

Slowly the colour flooded over Goldfinger's face. He stood, his mouth working, looking from the balls to Bond and back to the balls.

Bond said, softly, 'Too bad we were playing to the rules. Afraid that means you lose the hole. And, of course, the match.' Bond's eyes observed Goldfinger impassively.

'But, but . . .'

This was what Bond had been looking forward to—the cup dashed from the lips. He stood and waited, saying nothing.

Rage suddenly burst Goldfinger's usually relaxed face like a bomb. 'It was a Dunlop Seven you found in the rough. It was your caddie that give me this ball. On the seventeenth green. He gave me the wrong ball on purpose, the damned che—'

'Here, steady on,' said Bond mildly. 'You'll get a slander action on your hands if you aren't careful. Hawker, did you give Mr. Goldfinger the wrong ball by mistake or anything?'

'No, sir.' Hawker's face was stolid. He said indifferently, 'If you want my opinion, sir, the mistake may have been made at the seventeenth when the gentleman found his ball pretty far off the line we'd all marked it on. A Seven looks very much like a One. I'd say that's what happened, sir. It would have been a miracle for the gentleman's ball to have ended up as wide as where it was found.'

'Tommy rot!' Goldfinger gave a snort of disgust. He turned angrily on Bond. 'You saw that was a Number One my caddie found.'

Bond shook his head doubtfully. 'I didn't really look closely, I'm afraid. However,' Bond's voice became brisk, businesslike, 'it's really the job of the player to make certain he's using the right ball, isn't it? I can't see that anyone else can be blamed if you tee the wrong ball up and play three shots with it. Anyway,' he started walking off the green, 'many thanks for the match. We must have it again one day.'

Goldfinger, lit with glory by the setting sun, but with a long black shadow tied to his heels, followed Bond slowly, his eyes fixed thoughtfully on Bond's back.

Ian Fleming wrote about such sports as card playing, auto racing, and golf in his many Bond books.

ARNOLD PALMER

ARNOLD PALMER, 1968 P.G.A.

Alistair Cooke

It was 102 degrees and the wet winds from the Gulf of Mexico were drenching everybody from the eyebrows to the balls of the feet, when Arnold Palmer pulled a long-iron into the small Sahara of a bunker on the eighteenth hole of the Pecan Valley Country Club in San Antonio, Texas.

A long, low groan fanned over this mangrove swamp, in which the Professional Golf Association of America chose, God knows why, to play its fiftieth annual tournament. The groan came from Arnie's panting army, which through the long summer of his discontent has made more agonized sounds than the French going home from Moscow.

But Arnold had birdied the seventeenth hole and on the previous two he had been within a whisker of sinking two birdie putts that would have evened his score for three rounds and put him in the lead for the only one of the big four championships (the Masters, the US Open, the British Open, and the PGA) he has never won.

Now he loped down the fairway with wet circles under the arms of his flypaper shirt, and smaller rings in the wrinkles of his forehead. He looked at the poached egg of his ball in the deep sand. Wearily he took a mid-iron.

It was 120 yards to the flag and offered the sort of preposterous recovery that Palmer in the old, audacious days would have gone for and got. He mimicked the necessary lazy swing and the quick break of the wrists. He dropped his head and took a bead on the invisible rim of the poached egg. And he blasted.

The egg ballooned into a glistening white ball and it shot from a barrage of white sand and took a low trajectory over the intervening rough and the concrete fairway and the coarse fringe and it bounced on the green and plopped into the hole against the flag and rebounded an inch beyond the rim.

The empty sky was filled with a roar, the like of which has not been heard since he birdied the ninth hole at San Francisco two years ago in the US Open, and was seven strokes up at the turn. Palmer was Arnie again, the duffer's idol who makes the kind of recovery the duffer makes in dreams.

It was enough to send him in to an ocean of cheering and put him at the start today only two strokes behind the taut little gorilla known as Marty Fleckman and Frank Beard, the spectacled swinger—the new generation to whom a long, hot summer is the name of the game and Palmer is an old hero about to be buried in the record books.

Nothing has been more obvious or more comfortable to forget, in the recent US Open at Rochester, and the current joust

in the pecan country, than the muscular youngsters knocking on the door of the fortress where Palmer and Nicklaus and
Casper live. Lee Trevino, the young Mexican, turned Rochester into a pop Waterloo, where the old guard with their long
arcs and basic swings and all the panoply of the classic strategy were put to rout by an upstart with a baseball swing, a gab-
ble of jokes and a ditch-digger's putting stroke.

Just behind Trevino was Bert Yancey, the last walking ghost
of Bobby Jones, maintaining to the end the beautiful turn, the
pause at the top, the falling right shoulder and the graceful
sweep through that is now about to be anachronized before an
onslaught of young guys with the forearms of apes who ram
the ball into the air and rap it into the hole and know one
thing and one thing well: that whether you slug or scramble,
the low score takes the moneybag.

To this historic breakthrough there was added yesterday,
and the day before, and again today, the needle of the heat. It
turned the knife in the wound of the oldsters' humiliation.
Julius Boros, looking like a whipped Arab general, missed a
putt of three inches and almost slumped into the hole after it.
Tall, calm Weiskopf blew up at a news photographer.

Palmer had a blinding headache on Friday and sent out for
a hat: 'Not, for God's sake, a visor' — he still has some pride left
and a baseball visor is for baseball players. Yesterday Palmer
had 'puffy hands' and other veterans complained that in their
greasy hands the club felt no firmer than a snake.

There was a general call for salt tablets, and Trevino, who
thrives on sweat as a Scotsman on a keen west wind, grabbed
a pill just for the heck of it. He threw up. Never heard such
nonsense. He went back to his usual therapy of quick, short
strides and incessant gags, and his usual tactic of missing the
greens, shovelling up the short pitches, and ramming home
the long putts.

And where does this get him against Palmer's graceful heroics? Identical score, that's where: 212, two strokes off the lead.

At the blistering end of the day when there was no wind at all, and the sun glowered like an approaching comet, the youngsters heaved and chuckled around the locker room, and the traditional heroes went for footbaths and their memories were of mellower days and a slower pace.

Today is Palmer's great chance to retrieve the game for the old guard. If he fails,* he might well imitate the memorable San Francisco millionaire, a dogged old golfer, who pulled his drive, topped his wood shot, fluffed in the bunker, and took a small divot on the putting green! He straightened up and looked at his towering companions in utter amazement.

'What am I doing?' he cried, 'I don't *have* to do this. I'm a rich man!'

*He did.

Alistair Cooke, best known as the host of Masterpiece Theater, *is still one of the world's best sports journalists. This selection is taken from* Fun & Games with Alistair Cooke, *1994.*

LET IT BE RECORDED: McQUITTY NEVER QUIT

Mike Downey

Turnberry, Scotland—W.J. Robinson, a club pro from Kent hit a tee shot on the 18th hole at St. Margaret's-at-Cliffe on June 13, 1934. A cow crossed the fairway. The ball conked the cow on the head. The cow staggered 50 yards and dropped dead.

Robinson still had a better day than Guy McQuitty.

Harry Bradshaw hit a ball into a broken beer bottle at the British Open of 1949. He got conflicting rulings on whether the lie was unplayable, so he swung at the bottle. The ball flew out.

He still played better than Guy McQuitty.

Bernhard Langer's ball wedged in the branches of a tree at the Benson and Hedges Invitational in York, England. Langer shinnied up the trunk, stood in the fork of the tree and hit the ball out. Probably used a tree-iron.

And he still did better than Guy McQuitty.

Nigel Denham was finishing the first round of the English Open at Moortown in 1974. His shot hopped past the 18th green, went up the steps into the clubhouse and came to rest in the bar. He opened a window and pitched the ball onto the green, 12 feet from the pin.

Susan Rowlands was about to putt in the 1978 Welsh girls' championship at Abergate. A mouse ran up her pants leg. She holed the putt. The mouse ran down.

The Duke of Windsor once played a round on the Jinja course in Uganda. He was allowed to lift a ball out of a hippopotamus footprint without penalty. Course rules were fair this way, also saying: "If a ball comes to rest in dangerous proximity to a crocodile, another ball may be dropped."

If only Guy McQuitty had a good excuse, as those golfers did. Something that interfered with him. Animals, minerals, vegetables. Anything.

But, no. He only had one real explanation for why he shot 95 in the first round of the 1986 British Open, and 87 in the second round.

He played lousy.

At least Mike Reasor had a bum shoulder when he shot 123 and 114 in the final rounds of the 1974 Tallahassee Open. Any player who made the cut there automatically qualified for the following week's tournament. But you had to finish all four days. Reasor, who got hurt between rounds, wanted that exemption, so he kept playing.

Guy McQuitty is no quitter, but he doesn't have to be. He is done. Boy, is he ever done. Stick a fork in him.

After it had taken him 95 strokes to finish the opening round, McQuitty came back for more. But by the first tee, he was shaking. "I was scared to stand over the ball," he said.

The 23-year-old Englishman had carded two pars on Turnberry's first 18 holes. The only greens he hit in regulation were plants, leaves and passing green automobiles. "I lost all concentration after awhile," he said. "I couldn't even visualize how to swing the club."

There had been precedent for giving up. In 1935 at Muirfield, an unknown Scotsman opened his British Open with 7, 10, 5, 10. It took him 65 to reach the ninth cup. He took another 10 at the 11th. At the 12th, he hit into a bunker, tried four times to hit it out, then walked away.

Even while McQuitty was struggling last Thursday, a countryman named Andrew Broadway found himself at 57 after 10 holes. Broadway withdrew. But McQuitty would not. Club members back home at Exeter had financed his trip. "I couldn't let them down," he said, in the quote of the tournament.

He played the first nine Friday in 47, even getting a birdie on the fourth hole. That put him 37 over par for the Open.

McQuitty did not exactly draw a crowd for the back nine, but a photographer aimed a camera at him. "Want my picture?" McQuitty yelled. He ducked into a baseball catcher's squat and covered his head with both hands, like someone who had noticed the sky falling.

He saw every inch of Turnberry. Traps, weeds, trees, creeks . . . portable washrooms, too, probably. Certainly every grain of sand. Coming down the 17th fairway, a greenskeeper, rake over his shoulder, followed a few steps behind McQuitty, not letting him out of his sight.

At the 18th, McQuitty, by that time 42 over par, approached the green. There was polite applause. He waved and smiled. Might as well have been Nicklaus at Augusta. When he rolled in a putt, a spectator asked McQuitty's caddy:

"Does that give him a par?" The caddy replied: "He's parred the last four, actually."

Darned if he hadn't. McQuitty's final four holes were 3, 4, 5, 4. He was in the groove.

Later, on the clubhouse steps, the apple-cheeked blonde with the faintest mustache stood bravely and recounted his effort.

"Did you lose many balls?" he was asked.

"Oh, how many did we lose?" McQuitty said, consulting his caddy. "Twenty? Thirty?" He was laughing.

"Ever consider quitting?"

"Well," he said, "at one point I thought, you know, 'I wish I weren't here. This course is beating me up.' But that's a silly thing to say. I just told myself, 'Well, might as well keep going.'"

His total score was 182. There once was a British Open player named George Ritchie who shot 87-84—and still beat Guy McQuitty's score by 11 shots.

Ten years ago, an Englishman named Maurice Flitcroft, a crane operator, wanted to play in the British Open. He entered the first round of the qualifying event and shot 121. Tournament officials later discovered he had never played 18 holes of golf in his life. They sent him back his entry fee.

Guy McQuitty is a professional golfer. They intend to keep his.

Mike Downey is a trenchant and witty columnist for the Los Angeles Times. *This piece appeared July 20, 1986.*

ANNIKA SORENSTAM, 1996 U.S. WOMEN'S OPEN

Jim Burnett

Carrying a lead into the final rounds of the U.S. Open is the toughest challenge in sports.

The best in the game, the bravest and strongest have buck-led—Sam Snead, Arnold Palmer, Mickey Wright, Patty Sheehan. Talented players—Gil Morgan, who built a seven-stroke lead at Pebble Beach in 1992, Helen Alfredsson, who confidently opened up a seven-shot margin on the field at Indianwood in 1994—have watched in horror, almost trans-fixed, as the relentless pressure, tightening and tightening minute-by-minute, suddenly cracked them like a soft-boiled egg, spilling runny, yellow nerve endings all over the fairway.

ANNIKA SORENSTAM

"You don't win the Open: It wins you," said Cary Middlecoff, alluding to the fact that many Opens fall into the victor's lap. Final-round heroics, such as Johnny Miller's 63 in 1973 or Patty Sheehan's birdie-birdie finish in 1992, are incredibly rare.

But the woman of steel has already bought her ticket to the biggest, scariest Fun House of them all, and looks forward to the journey. "I don't mind being chased," she tells the media. "I think it's a good experience, and I've got to be able to handle this too. You cannot always chase someone. I think it's important to be able to hold the lead, also. You learn a lot from that, and that's the way golf is. You've got to be able to adjust to every situation."

At any rate, with her sun-bleached blonde hair, gold engagement band, gold earrings, slender gold bracelet—and a three-stroke lead—Sorenstam certainly *looks* golden.

In the 1960s it was Arnie's army.

In the late 1970s and 1980s it was Nancy's navy.

In the 1990s, at a site once used for an air force base it can only be Annika's air force. And the fans are out in full force. From the back of the crowd around the 1st green, it's barely possible to see the top of Sorenstam's black Callaway cap.

The early holes follow a familiar pattern. Burton, dressed in a light purple shirt with cream trim and cream shorts, scrambles from the rough. Sorenstam hits nothing but fairways and greens.

Burton has been working with Senior Tour star Dave Stockton on her short game since January and talking to him every night this week. Stockton is one of the finest putters in the game, a magician with the flat stick, and he seems to have passed his gift to Burton, who has sunk a career's worth of long putts this year. Maybe it's one of those Vulcan, or Stockton, Mind Meld things. On the 127-yard 3rd hole, Burton snakes home a 25-footer for birdie; Sorenstam, repulsing the early challenge, trumps it with a 7-footer of her own.

For the golfers, hemmed in by writers, photographers, cameramen and microphones, and surrounded by dense packs of fans, it's almost like swinging in a phone booth, with a bunch of faces pressed up against the glass.

"God, I hope I don't kill anybody," murmurs Burton, as she yanks a long iron toward the crowd. She winds up in the pine straw and works hard to salvage bogey.

Sorenstam gets her first test of the day: a three-foot putt on a spiked-up green. Although she rotates her head when swinging her woods and irons, Sorenstam anchors it when she putts, waiting to hear the sound of the ball plunking into the cup. She does, the crowd applauds, and Sorenstam offers a tense "thank you."

On the 393-yard 6th hole, Sorenstam hooks her drive into the second cut of rough. It's one of only five fairways she will miss in the entire tournament, and it brings an exasperated frown. After playing safely short of the green, Sorenstam pitches nicely to four feet.

No little Annika smiles now. She looks tense, perhaps a bit scared, as she fidgets over the par putt. But her stroke is bulletproof.

"She has the game and the temperament suited for this kind of pressure," Jane Geddes will say later. "She is so precise, so poised, way beyond her years. Catching her today was a thought some of us had. But that was all it was—a thought." Her opposition is treading water. Sorenstam holds a commanding five-stroke lead over Burton and Geddes.

Like all great players, Sorenstam is an inveterate scoreboard watcher. As Johnny Miller puts it, "In the heat of a major championship, it's a jungle out there, and when there's a noise, the small animals look for cover while the lions find out what caused it. They're not afraid of anything.

"Jack Nicklaus was that way. So was Arnold Palmer. . . . They were kings of the jungle."

When Sorenstam sees she is firmly in command, she seems to relax a little. With 220 yards to the pin on the 440-yard 10th hole, from a sidehill lie with the ball above her feet, Sorenstam scorches a magnificent 3-wood which rolls up 20 feet from the cup. When she slam-dunks the eagle putt, she raises both hands overhead, breaks into a high-beam smile that lights up the roaring gallery, and floats from the green to the next tee on waves of applause. Up ahead Kris Tschetter, in the process of shooting a 66 that will sweep her into second place, sees Sorenstam move to eight under par, and says to herself, "What golf course is *she* playing?"

"This isn't a golf tournament," says a fan watching Annika's air force, worshipping in her wake, "It's a coronation."

Even the cautious, conservative, play-it-as-it-lies, take-nothing-for-granted USGA agrees. As Sorenstam cruises through No. 12 with a seven-shot lead, it does something astonishing, not to mention unprecedented. It issues a press release which reads:

"Annika Sorenstam's winning 72-hole total of 2 [sic] is a new U.S. Women's Open scoring record. . . . [Sorenstam] is only the sixth woman to have won back-to-back U.S. Open titles."

As if to remind everyone she's human, Sorenstam bogeys Nos. 13 and 14. But she birdies No. 15, and then, on the 172-yard 16th hole, turns a coronation into an exhibition for the ages. Armed with a 6-iron, she pulls the trigger on a rifle shot that almost literally knocks the pin down—the ball takes one bounce and clangs off the flagstick. Sorenstam can't see it—she doesn't wear her contacts on breezy days—but the screams from the crowd around the green reverberate all the way back to the tee box.

And the mind flashes to the exploits of another great athlete, Annie Oakley, when she coolly blasted targets from the sky in front of 30,000 cheering fans. A prim, proper lady, a bit of a loner offstage, and a dazzling, steely-willed competitor of almost otherworldly skill and poise onstage. Years later 39,000 cheering fans shake the heavens with applause as Sorenstam walks down the 18th Fairway and into the history books. Her final round 66 ties the record for lowest final round at the U.S. Open; her 72-hole total of 272 shatters the previous mark of 277 set by Liselotte Neumann in 1988, when Sorenstam sat up all night, glued to the tube, dreaming a teenager's dreams about following in her countrywoman's footsteps.

PATTY SHEEHAN, 1996 DINAH SHORE

Jim Burnett

An outstanding athlete—Sheehan was a potential Olympic skier until she gravitated toward golf at the age of 13—Sheehan burst onto the Tour in 1981 after a fine college career at San Jose State.

Small but strong, the five-foot-three Sheehan seemed to have a physique manufactured for golf—a slim, graceful upper body resting on ski-slope muscled thighs that a female middle linebacker would envy. With a swing reminiscent of Ben Hogan and the feisty energy and athleticism of a Gary Player, Sheehan attacked courses with the relentless persistence of a terrier.

PATTY SHEEHAN

Sheehan won early and often—the LPGA Championship in 1982 and 1983 and 18 other tournaments in the 1980's. But she seemed to lose some of her lust for battle as the decade wore on.

The five-minute delay on the tee at 18 is excruciating. With the cameraman in her face again, Sheehan towels off, stretches her neck from side to side, stretches out her quad muscles, waits, and waits some more.

Professional golfers who have played other sports pinpoint the wait between shots as the key element that makes golf so agonizing. In the mirrors of the Fun House, time is distorted into slow motion: seconds drip down like an exquisite Chinese water torture, playing havoc with the mind. The Fun House is more than a metaphor. A *Golf Digest* article in 1994 detailed the physiological effects of nervousness, the times when " your body can turn into a stranger." The effects include soaring blood pressure, accelerated heartbeat and respiratory rate; blood flowing from the extremities to the brain and torso, resulting in cold, stiff hands and fingers; the digestive system shutting down, resulting in stomach, bowls and bladder trying to empty; secretion of endorphins that can result in numbness; blood, oxygen and nutrients pouring to the brain, which at first enhances thinking but soon, when the brain can no longer process the nutrients, produces confusion.

In her amateur days, Lopez used to "throw up in the morning, throw up on the way to the course, and throw up at the golf club." Bobby Jones lost up to 18 pounds in a single tournament, concentrating so deeply he burned calories like a marathon runner. Afterward his hands often shook so badly he could only remove his necktie by cutting it off.

Ellsworth Vines, the top U.S. tennis player in the 1930's before becoming a fine professional golfer, once said, "In tennis you seldom have a chance, once things get going, to get shaky. You're too busy running around like a racehorse. But in golf—hell, it makes me nervous just to talk about it. That little white ball just sits there. A man can beat himself before he ever swings at it."

Up ahead the great green whale continues to wreak havoc.

"Nobody wants it," says Dee Darden, photographing from the 18th fairway. Robbins, whose second shot lands in deep rough, has to lay up short of the pond, then misses a beautifully struck par putt that curls around the high side of the cup. Sorenstam, in perfect position in two, boldly attacks the flag, located in the back right corner of the huge green, but can't hold the slick putting surface with a wedge. Her four-foot par spins around and out of the cup. Mallon, who knocked the pin down on the closing holes but couldn't buy a putt, misses a six-foot birdie effort. All three finish at six under par. Although Sheehan doesn't yet know it, she's back in the lead.

No one wins a major championship without a break or two along the way. Sheehan pulls her drive toward the lake and stares in agony as the ball descends to earth.

"Oh, don't go in the water," she prays out loud.

"Is it wet?" yells a fan.

"Oh, it's fine!" says another.

Barely. Sheehan gets lucky, the ball coming to rest a few yards away from a watery grave. Maybe the golfing gods, high up in their viewing box—maybe Dinah herself, who once nicknamed Sheehan "Mighty Mite"—used a bit of celestial body English.

As Sheehan prepares to hit her second shot, the Caddie Machine, who has caught a glimpse of the scoreboard back by the 17th tee, decides it's time for a conference.

"Patty, can I tell you something?"

"What?"

"You're leading."

"I know I'm leading," says Sheehan, thinking she'd tied for the top spot.

"No," says Laib. " You're leading."

Meanwhile Nause is playing her second shot from the right rough. She pushes a fairway wood, and with a huge gallery gathered around her, Nause yells at the top of her lungs.

"Hook!!! Damn it!!!"

What a game golf is! Five hours ago Nause was as confident, collected, and composed as a news anchor on a good hair day. Now she's a raw nerve ending, her overstuffed black bag of anger splitting at the seams. Maybe she can get a sports psychologist referral from Burton, who has retained her equanimity despite her ball-striking struggles and back pains.

Sheehan pushes her second shot into a fairway bunker. She has 116 yards over the lake to a pin tucked in the back right corner of the green, a shot that would terrify most golfers. But for Sheehan, it's a comfortable 9-iron.

It comes out dead left, however. Sheehan is left with a monstrous putt of about 120 feet over a big ridge.

Robbins and Mallon sit on their golf bags just across the island green, on an incline underneath the scorer's tent, joking and readying themselves for a playoff. Sorenstam sits nearby with fiancé David Esch. Webb, who finished at five under par, after rimming out a 20-foot birdie try at the 18th, hangs around to soak in the drama.

It couldn't be a tougher two-putt. As is her wont in such situations, Sheehan gives herself a little pep talk. "C'mon! You're a good player! Don't let this slip away!" From a vantage point at the back of the green, Sheehan is so far away, and the ridge bisecting the green is so steep, it's impossible to see the lower part of her body.

With the whole golf world watching, and the crowd as hushed as church mice, Sheehan raps the putt over the ridge and watches at it funnels down to within six feet of the cup, a brilliant effort. Still, none of the contenders have made a putt from this distance all day. If she misses—and Burton sinks her 15-foot birdie putt—a five-way playoff will ensue.

Burton's brave bid slides by the cup.

Sheehan paces the green and studies the putt from every angle. Then she crouches down, hands cupped around her visor, and takes a deep breath. "You've done this thousands of times before," she tells herself. "So go ahead and do it again."

Curtis Strange once called Nancy Lopez " the best putter in the world from eight feet in, man, woman, or child." The best clutch putter in golf, in recent years, has been Patty Sheehan. And she's performed seeming miracles—such as finishing birdie, birdie at the 1992 U.S. Open—with the same weapon she's carried since she's turned pro, a Wilson 8802 model with a silver blade as nicked-up as the putters handed out at a miniature golf course.

As she takes her stance, Sheehan's cool concentration is palpable. Sorenstam can feel it as well. "It's going in," she whispers to her fiancé Esch.

The putt is struck so purely that Sheehan begins to straighten and shout and jump for joy before the ball rolls into the heart of the cup. A mighty roar erupts from the grandstand, flooding over Sheehan like a tsunami. Sheehan once turned a somersault after winning a tournament in Japan. A few days ago, in a practice round, she tried a cartwheel. Now, at her mother's request, she performs a nifty one on the edge of the green as the crowd continues to stand and cheer.

ABC, almost out of airtime, collars her for a quick interview. " I'd like to dedicate this to my dad," says Sheehan. " He's not been feeling that well lately."

"Water! Water! Water!" the fans yell, and reluctant Sheehan, clutching a huge, silver four-foot trophy and a bouquet of roses, finally obliges, wading back and forth across the waist-high water, the green monster vanquished.

Jim Burnett is a regular contributor to Golf *magazine.* Tee Times, *from which this excerpt comes, appeared in 1997.*

HALE IRWIN,
1990 U.S. OPEN

Dave Anderson

'As Sweet as a Baby's Kiss'
Medinah, Ill.

Hale Irwin had shot 67 for 280, jogging a victory lap around the 18th green under a warm waterfall of applause after holing a 45-foot putt to finish the 90th United States Open at eight under par. And now, as the 45-year-old touring pro answered questions in the interview tent, he politely refused to discuss what his feelings would be if he were to win his third Open.

"I'm not winning this tournament at the moment," he said. "Until that time I don't want to discuss that."

HALE IRWIN

Just then the two-time Open champion noticed the assembled reporters reacting to what was happening on a television screen he couldn't see.

"What happened?" he said. "I want a blow-by-blow."

"Donald saved par with a long putt," he was told.

In the wind that finally blew across Medinah's No. 3 course, the leaderboard watchers had focused on Curtis Strange's bid for a third consecutive Open title, on Nick Faldo's bid to keep a Grand Slam alive, on Jack Nicklaus and Greg Norman. But almost invisibly Mike Donald, a 35-year-old touring pro who only a few years ago was delivering flowers, kept making or saving pars for a 71 that would create an 18-hole playoff with Hale Irwin today.

No matter which golfer wins, this Open will be remembered for Irwin's 45-foot birdie putt across the grassy hump of the 18th green, a shot that took an uncanny 6.3 seconds to find its way into the cup.

"I hung it out there to break about five feet, and it trickled right down in, as sweet as a baby's kiss," said the father of two teen-age daughters. "In my 22 years on the tour, I've never made a putt like that to win or come close to winning. It was easily four times any putt I made all week. I'm not going to say it was purely accidental, but the hole got in the way."

In today's playoff, experience will favor Irwin, a two-time Open champion who won at Winged Foot in 1974 and at Inverness in 1979. If he were to win today in golf's only 18-hole playoff, he would be the only golfer with three United States Open championships except for the four men who each won four: Jack Nicklaus, Ben Hogan, Bobby Jones and Willie Anderson.

"That's a different format," Irwin said of the playoff. "To stay as high as I am now might be difficult."

On yesterday's back nine, Irwin finally felt comfortable putting, holing five birdie putts for a 31.

"When I got to eight under with that last putt," Irwin said, "I didn't think I won the Open, but I knew I'd have a chance to win the Open. With only eight holes to go, I was only three under. So to get to eight under was the exhilaration. Not that I expected to win, but I expected to have a chance."

Upon entering the interview tent, Irwin did an encore of his victory lap: jogging down an aisle, past the front of the platform where he would sit, up another aisle, then turning and hurrying up behind the table where he would sit.

"I don't know how you can remain stoic after making a putt like that," Irwin said. "Had I done something like that without a soul watching, I would've been happy. But with that roar ringing in your ears, it was really something."

Seldom has a golfer reacted so emotionally to a memorable putt. Some golfers wave. Some do a quick dance. Some hug their caddie.

But knowing he might have an opportunity to be the oldest Open champion, Irwin, his arms high, jogged across and around the green, then high-fived a few of the gallery marshalls. He did everything but spike his putter. With that in mind, the former University of Colorado defensive back was asked if he had ever celebrated like that after an interception.

"I never had any," he said with a laugh.

"But if there was a moment in this round," Irwin said, "it was the 10-foot putt I made at the ninth for a par. I needed something there to stabilize myself. Starting at the 11th, I made four straight birdies with three close iron shots to six feet, four feet and three feet, and a wedge to four feet."

And he had done it at Medinah No. 3 in a wind that you could see, hear and feel. See it fluttering the blades of grass tossed into the sky by the golfers. Hear it howling through the leaves of the towering trees. Feel it gusting across your face.

Finally, the wind was up yesterday just in time for the final round. The wind that blows fly balls into home runs at Wrigley Field, for Cubs and opponents alike. The wind that once blew a football away from the right foot of the Giants' punter, Sean Landeta, in a pro football playoff game.

The same wind that yesterday blew Hale Irwin into an 18-hole playoff for what might be his third Open title after a 45-foot birdie putt as sweet as a baby's kiss.

JUNE 18, 1990

If it had been the Masters, the Professional Golfers Association Championship or any of hundreds of golf tournaments all over the world, Mike Donald would have won the sudden-death playoff with a 4-foot birdie putt at the first hole.

If it had been the British Open, Hale Irwin would have won the four-hole playoff by one stroke.

But this was the United States Open, the only major golf tournament that insists upon the integrity of the 18-hole play-off. And so Hale Irwin, two strokes behind going to the 16th tee, finally emerged yesterday as the oldest Open champion at the age of 45 with an 8-foot birdie putt on the 19th hole that polished to a high gloss the tradition of the 18-hole playoff.

"I just kept pecking away," Irwin said later.

As any golfer knows, "pecking away" is what the game is all about. Pecking away over 18 holes, not for one hole or two or maybe four in a sudden-death format. If you're all tied after 18 holes, that's different. Mike Donald had a 15-foot par putt to win at the 18th on Medinah's No. 3 course. But when he missed it, they returned to the first tee to the first sudden-death situation in Open history.

With his birdie putt at the 19th hole, Irwin earned his third Open title, the only golfer with that many except for the four who each have won four: Jack Nicklaus, Ben Hogan, Bobby Jones and Willie Anderson.

Dave Anderson is the distinguished sports columnist for the New York Times.

NICK FALDO, 1993 RYDER CUP

―――――――――

John Feinstein

It was 7:55 the next morning when the carts carrying Azinger, Couples, Faldo, and Montgomerie pulled up to the 18th tee. It was overcast, but at least there was no fog. It was also freezing. The official temperature reading at 8 o'clock was 49 degrees with gusty winds. Everyone knew what was at stake, including the fans who had already turned out in force and had started jostling for position at sunrise.

Montgomerie hit first, pushing a weak but safe shot into the right rough. With his partner dry, Faldo was able to aim down the left and bite off a large chunk of the water. For a split second, it looked as if he had bitten off too much. But the ball

RYDER CUP TROPHY

landed safely in the left fairway and a huge cheer went up as the ball bounced into the view of the gallery.

Couples led off for the Americans. The minute his ball left the club it was dead. It started left and hooked. It splashed into the water as another cheer went up. One American down, one to go.

Azinger had not been this nervous during his PGA playoff a month earlier against Greg Norman. He *had* to get the ball into the fairway in position to reach the green. He couldn't let Faldo win the hole with a par and put the Europeans two points up.

He was shaking with nerves and the cold. "My Florida bones can't take that kind of cold," he said. "When I saw Freddy's ball get wet, I thought, Oh boy, it's all on me now."

Under the circumstances, the shot may have been as good as any Azinger has ever hit. It flew on almost the same line as Faldo's ball, landed in the fairway, and rolled 15 yards beyond Faldo. The crowd applauded appreciatively, knowing a great shot under pressure when it saw one.

"Great tee shot," Watson said, his hands stuffed in his pockets to ward off the cold.

They made their way up the fairway. Montgomerie was first to play. From a bad lie, he hit his ball weakly into the water. Groans. Faldo, standing behind his ball in the fairway, showed no emotion at all. Mentally though, he flinched.

God, now it's one against one, he thought. I bloody well better hit this one well and put some pressure on Azinger.

He didn't. His seven-iron shot reached the green well short of the pin. Watson walked up next to him. "Great tee shot," he said again.

Azinger stood behind his ball for what seemed like forever, tossing grass into the air to check the wind over and over. He and his caddy, Mark Jiminez, finally decided on an eight-iron. The shot was almost perfect. It landed pin high, but just a tad right—about 18 feet from the flag.

Advantage, U.S.

The other twenty players, having finished their warm-ups for the matches that would begin at 8:30, were now sitting greenside. Couples and Montgomerie, both now spectators too, joined them. The green, the stage and pendulum of the match, belonged to Azinger and Faldo.

Their rivalry stretched back to 1987, when Azinger had bogeyed the last two holes of the British Open to give Faldo a one-shot victory and his first major title. Azinger had carried that wound with him for years. It had been exacerbated when Faldo was quoted as making fun of Azinger's unorthodox grip. During the last round of the PGA when Azinger had seen Faldo's name of the top of the leader board along with his and Norman's, his resolve had seemed to double.

"It was nothing personal, he claimed. "But I didn't want to lose another major to *him*."

He didn't. Now the two men were face-to-face in a totally different situation. Each was a millionaire and there wasn't a penny at stake. But both could feel the almost unbearable tension as they walked onto the 18th green. Their teammates were yelling encouragement, but neither man heard a word.

Faldo putted first. The 18th was probably the slowest green on the golf course, especially early in the morning. Faldo knew it was slow, but not how slow, and his putt stopped 10 feet short. No one on the American team thought for one second that he would miss the second putt, no matter how difficult it might be.

They were all hoping that Azinger would make Faldo's putt irrelevant. He walked around the ball, lining it up from all angles. Kneeling nearby, Watson heard a TV technician's walkie-talkie crackle.

His head snapped around. "Turn that thing down!" he demanded.

Azinger's putt looked like it was in until it got to within a yard of the hole, when it started to slide just right. Azinger threw his head back, his eyes closed, and let out a deep sigh of frustration. He walked up and tapped the ball in for par.

The Americans could do no worse than tie. If Faldo somehow missed, the first day's play would end 4-4 *and* the U.S. would start day two with a full head of steam. But Faldo's putt was never going anywhere but dead center. The crowd screamed for joy and the Europeans surrounded him on the green. Europe was ahead, 4½-3½.

Faldo grabbed Torrance's hand as if he was going to fall over. "What's for breakfast?" he said. Then his knees buckled and he bent over and let out a huge sigh of relief.

NICK PRICE,
1994 BRITISH OPEN

John Feinstein

Two men were left with a chance. One was Parnevik, who, after Watson's collapse, had put on the first real charge of the day, birdieing three straight holes, bogeying one, then birdieing two more. That got him to 12 under par with one hole to play.

It also seemed to put him in control of the tournament. The only player even within hailing distance of him was Price, and he was struggling. He had started slowly like everyone else, making three-putt bogeys on two and five, the second one from 25 feet.

Seeing that his boss was as angry as he ever got, Squeeky Medlen, Price's caddy, said softly as they walked off the sixth tee, "That just stoked the fire, Nick. Let's go."

Slowly, they went. Price finally got a birdie at the seventh and hung in. But when he got to the 13th and found himself trailing Parnevik by three, he began to wonder if this wasn't going to be another opportunity lost.

"I was too careful the first five or six holes," he said. "I was trying not to put a foot wrong, and that's not the way to play. I had to just *play*."

He did, but Parnevik had gotten so hot it appeared it might be too little, too late. The Nick Price of the 1980s might have looked at Parnevik's number on the board and thought, oh well, too good, well played, let's see if we can't get second. But the Nick Price of the 1990s never thinks a tournament is over. He always thinks there may just be a way to pull it out.

He had to wave par from behind the green at 13. Then at 14, he caught a flyer in the rough and hit his second shot way over the green. A bogey would finish him, he knew that. He got lucky that he was so far over the green that he was in a trampled-down area and had a decent lie. He hit a running seven-iron that skidded to a halt three feet past the pin. Relieved, he tapped in for par. He was still nine under, Parnevik, 11. He hit a good five-iron at the par-three 15th, but his 18-foot putt spun past. Walking up 16, Price heard a roar and knew Parnevik had birdied 17. Somehow, he had to make a birdie.

He did, knocking a sand wedge to 12 feet and making the putt. Parnevik was at 12 under, he was at 10. The 17th was eminently reachable in two. If he could birdie it and birdie 18 . . . there was still a chance.

Up ahead, Parnevik was doing his Ernie Els imitation. He had decided not to look at any leader boards and had ordered his caddy not to tell him anything. Hearing various shouts and cheers behind him, he somehow figured that he was either behind or tied as he stood on the 18th tee. In truth, since Price was still on 16 at that moment, he was leading by three.

He hit his tee shot to the right side of the fairway. If he had known he was leading, he would have played a four-iron to the middle of the green. But thinking he needed a birdie, he aimed a five-iron right at the flag, which was tucked front and left in an almost impossible spot to get close.

The shot sailed left into the gorse, a terrible spot. Parnevik flopped a good wedge shot out to within 10 feet, but missed the putt. He tapped in for bogey, a round of 67 and a total of 11 under. When someone told him that he had been leading by three, all the color drained out of his face.

The three-shot lead was down to one after the bogey and Price's birdie at 16. Price had crushed his drive at 17 and had a four-iron left to the green. He knocked it on, 50 feet past the flag. A two-putt birdie would tie him with Parnevik. A playoff suddenly loomed. As they walked onto the green, Medlen had a thought.

"You know, we haven't made a long one all week," he said.

Price glanced at the huge yellow scoreboard. Parnevik's bogey wasn't up yet. He thought he needed to make the eagle putt to tie. "I put every drop of blood I had into making that putt," he said.

The putt had very little break in it, only about eight inches, so speed was the key. As soon as Price saw it go over the crest of the little hill on the green, he could see that it was headed straight for the hole. "I wondered if it would hang on," he said.

About eight feet away, the ball took a tiny hop to the right— Price saw later watching it on tape that it had hit a spike mark— and for a split second he thought it might slip past the cup on the right side. But at the last possible second it hit the corner of the cup, spun around the edge briefly, and dropped.

Standing in the fairway waiting to play his second shot, Brad Faxon saw Price jump what looked to him like 20 feet straight into the air. "I was waiting for Squeeky to catch him, but then I saw him up in the air too," he said.

Faxon knew what had happened. The roar told everyone else. The putt was exactly 17 paces — 51 feet — long. By nightfall it would be described in various places around the world as between 70 and 80 feet long. In any event, it was the shot of the year.

When he came back to earth, Price looked at the leader board again. He was much too experienced *not* to look. He saw Parnevik's bogey. After seventy-one holes, for the first time all week, he had the lead. Now all he had to do was par the hole he had bogeyed the last two days. Where the hell was that seven-and-a-half-iron Leadbetter had talked about?

Price has had high blood pressure all his life. Now he took a few deep breaths to stay calm as he stood on the 18th tee. All he wanted to do was hit a three-iron around the corner and hope he ended up in a good spot to get to the middle of the green. He hit the shot solidly, but thought it might be a little farther left than he wanted it.

"It's fine," Medlen said as they walked off the tee. "The only thing I care about is that we're not between clubs again."

Price was thinking the same thing. When they got to the ball, the lie was fine. Medlen checked the yardage — 165! A seven-iron! No more, no less, exactly a seven-iron. "My favorite club, my favorite shot," Price said. "If I couldn't putt that shot on the green, I'd quit golf."

He took his time and the ball sailed directly at the center of the green — right where Parnevik should have aimed. When it landed, the crowd was screaming. Short of Watson, they could think of no one they would rather see win than Price.

As he began his walk to the green, Price felt chills racing through him. He had waited all his life to make this walk — to the 18th green at the Open championship, needing two putts to win. He started to say something to Medlen, but when he turned his head, he wasn't there. Thinking that Price deserved this moment to himself, Medlen had dropped behind him.

No way. Price turned to Medlen and waved him up. Medlen hesitated. "Come on, Squeek," Price said, "let's enjoy this together. Who knows if we'll ever get to do it again."

And so they walked onto the green together, both of them tingling. There were still 30 feet to negotiate, though, and Price suddenly flashed back to the three-putt at the fifth. "I didn't want to stand there taking all the bows and then make a fool of myself by three-putting," he said.

He didn't. He carefully lagged to three feet, looked the putt over, and tapped it in. He was in Medlen's arms, the two of them pounding one another for joy. Sue Price didn't really want to go out onto the green, she felt it was Nick's moment not hers, but her parents and their friends were pushing her and she finally went out there and Nick practically crushed her with his bear hug.

A few minutes later, at 6:18 P.M. on a sparkling summer evening, Charles Jack, the captain of Turnberry, introduced "the champion golfer of the year," and handed him the coveted claret jug. Price grabbed it in his huge hands and kissed it with all his might. "In 1982, I had my left hand on this trophy," he said. "In 1988, I had my right hand on it. Now, at last, I've got both hands on it."

John Feinstein is the author of such best selling sports books as A Season on the Brink, Play Ball, *and* Hard Courts. *These selections were taken from* A Good Walk Spoiled, *1995.*

DRIVES
AND WHISPERS

———————

Dan Jenkins

Talk about your pressure shots in golf! Only moments ago
on videotape, this was Severiano Ballesteros—ankle-deep in
quicksand, the green more than 260 yards away, the wind dead
against him as it howls in off the ocean here at the rugged but
scenic Realtor's Swamp Country Club. Not a very hopeful situation for the two-time winner of The Masters, but watch
what happens, golf fans! The determined Spaniard takes a
lusty swing with his 3-wood and—splat! The shot rises above
the tall, protruding palms. It clears the hotel and spa. It clears
the teeming hordes of hotpants and halter tops in the gallery.
Good bounce across the cart path—and on the green! And

now, as the drama continues to unfold, Seve Ballesteros has this birdie putt of about 27½ feet to go eight under through nine holes and grab the lead in today's fourth and final round of the Franchot Tone National Pro-Comedian, Singer, Car Dealer, Estate Planner, and Bank of Kowloon Knitwear Classic!

Good afternoon, ladies and gentlemen, I'm Don Void, and what a feast we have for you here on the beautiful northeast coast of Florida. The oilslick has disappeared, the red tide has receded, most of the condominiums have been refinanced, and it's all winding down to a climax in the third annual F.T.N.P.C.S.C.D.E.P.B.K.K.C., one of the truly great events on the PGA Tour and, I might mention, a tournament that's contributed more than $6 million to local charities, less expenses, advertising costs, promotional fees, and what have you.

I'm Don Void, as I said earlier, and working with me today on the 18th hole is my friend and cohort, Wristy Stark, the former PGA champion, probably the greatest chipper the game has ever known, and a guy who knows how to provide the lighter touch. We'll be looking forward to his comments throughout the telecast.

Right now, as Seve lines up his putt—there's a nice shot from our Goodyear blimp, Albatross, piloted today by Captain Stormy Werther of Lakehurst, New Jersey—let's catch you up on the action that took place on Thursday, Friday, and Saturday at this clambake-classic.

Arnold Palmer and Jack Nicklaus, magical names of course, stole the thunder on Thursday. Making a couple of those patented charges of theirs, they blazed in with 77s and shared the early lead. Talk about thrills! Before the day was over, however, the lead belonged to Howell Rowell Jr. and five other second-year pros, all tied with 10-under 62s. Among the group was Ed Fusilli. Here we see Ed's pretty wife, Rachel, asking him to examine a W-2 form.

Friday was the day young Brad Method made a move. The Houston rookie put a sizzling 61 on the scoreboard and leaped into a tie with Howell Rowell. Brad's pink polyesters flap in the breeze as he pulls the trigger on a 1-iron. There's Brad's wife, Debbie, showing us two reasons she once held the title of Miss Sioux Falls.

The wind kicked up on Saturday—there goes the press tent, as you can see—but the subpar rounds continued. Howell Rowell and Brad Method were still leading at the end of the day, but Ballesteros was close, and who could overlook Arnie and Big Jack, only 22 shots off the pace?

Fine camerawork there on Mrs. Brad Method, being helped with her troublesome halter top by tournament officials.

So we're up to date on all the scoring. Now let's go out on the course and meet the expert commentators who'll be helping me bring you all the live action. First to the 13th hole and Steve Gunch.

"Hello, I'm Steve Gunch. I'll be reporting from the two-hundred-twenty-seven-yard, par-three thirteenth hole, a severe test of the golfers' nerves. The green is bordered on three sides by waterfalls, but the biggest problem for the players, as I see it, is the reptile farm that comes right up to the front edge of the putting surface. I look for most of the fellows to go at it with a driver—try to bounce one off the synagogue behind the green. It's the percentage shot. And now to the fourteenth and our colleague from overseas, Peter Brace-Asher."

"Jolly good fun to be here, I must say. And my, what marvelous stuff we're seeing from all the lads as they nestle their wedges around this rather intoxicating marshland. As for the fourteenth, well, what a diabolical thing it is! One bloody slip, to my way of thinking, and you're consigned to a watery grave. On to the fifteenth, then."

"Hi, I'm Vern Utterance. I'll be describing the action here at the fifteenth, a six-hundred-three-yard par-five that—no, wait a minute, that's the sixteenth. Sorry. the fifteenth is a four-hundred-twenty-three-yard par-four that appears to have a good bit of grass in the fairway. From my vantage point, in fact, I can see grass all the way back to the tee. Over to sixteen."

"This is Frank Murk at the crowd-pleasing sixteenth hole, where we've seen thirty-eight pars, two hundred thirty-seven birdies, and forty-nine bogeys posted by golfers ranging in height from five feet five inches to six feet two inches with an average weight of one hundred sixty-five pounds. In addition, most of the touring pros from California and Texas were born there. That's the story from sixteen. Now over to seventeen and the colorful J. L. Starnes, who's just completed his round and agreed to join our announce crew today. Welcome aboard, J. L."

"Uh, this is J. L. Starnes. I'll tell you one thing. They can take this seventeenth hole and give it back to the goats. The summitch cost me about three grand a while ago. I drove it perfect, right down the left side, but I must have hit a sprinkler head or something. I wound up in the shit. Got on the green after I chipped out and cold-jumped a four wood, but the green's slicker'n Sam Snead's head, so I three-putt the cocksucker. Maybe I got what I deserved. Play the fucker like Mother Goose, you're gonna make six."

Right you are, J. L.! I'm Don Void back at the 18th where I've been informed by the studio that the basketball game is about to get under way. We'll be returning to the Franchot Tone for all the golf action after today's all-important contest between the Mavericks and the Suns. So for Steve Gunch, Peter Brace-Asher, Vern Utterance, Frank Murk, J. L. Starnes, and Wristy Stark, this is Don Void, saying so long from Realtor's Swamp!

Dan Jenkins is best known for such works as Semi-Tough, Baja Oklahoma, *and* Rude Behavior. "Drives and Whispers" *appeared in Playboy in 1985.*

WHAT WAS HE THINKING? (Jean Van de Velde, 1999 British Open)

Jeff Rude

Carnoustie, Scotland

What price glory? Jean Van de Velde knows now. French silk becomes burnt French toast. His happy romp turns to, in his words, "nightmare". Because he was not safe, he was sorry, undressed in full view and transformed into a tragic figure of sport.

"It's sad," the funny Frenchman said. "Very sad."

The passionate one had such a grip on the 128th British Open, the engraver started crafting his name for the claret jug. But then he suffers a mind cramp, errs on the side of his go-for-gusto culture, hits 2-iron instead of cautious wedge, finds himself in grassy and wet spots of bother, free-falls into a collapse for the ages, and now the scratch man has to erase and write in surprise beneficiary Paul Lawrie.

"I made a lot of friends because a Scottish man won," he said, gallows humorous to the end.

Van de Velde first embraced golf at age 6, on a miniature course in southwest France. "Goofy or adventure golf," he called it. So then, it follows, he started preparing for the borderline silly treachery of Carnoustie Golf Links 27 years ago. But then even dreamers from his Disneyland sponsor couldn't concoct the dramatic misfortune he suffered on the 72nd hole of the game's oldest championship.

One hole to play, three strokes ahead of Justin Leonard and Lawrie, each finished at 6-over-par 290. Double-bogey 6 wins for a pre-Open 150-1 shot. Just make double and maybe then the French discover there's more in life besides wine, cheese, romance, soccer and cycling.

But Van de Velde made a time-consuming triple bogey 7 and in the process spliced Tin Cup and Caddyshack into one flick. It was a tragicomedy that drew gasps and second-guesses, gave Lawrie and Leonard renewed hope for a playoff and sent historians rushing off to find this: He became the first Open 54-hole leader to blow a five-stroke advantage since someone named Jose Jurado of Argentina in 1931, also at Carnoustie.

"Usually he makes more than one stupid mistake on the golf course," said his wife, Brigitte, whom he met in pre-school. "This week he only made one."

Van de Velde's problems started at the 18th tee, when he thought he was ahead by two strokes, not three, and figured he needed bogey to win outright. His caddie, beret-wearing Christophe Angiolin, set him straight on the margin walking down the fairway, before they reached his tee ball, pushed with a driver far right to a cushy lie on the 17th hole.

Living a happy life or posting good golf scores, of course, is all about making good decisions. Next, Van de Velde made a highly questionable call and got an outrageously unlucky break you wouldn't wish on an adversary. Faced with 189 yards to carry Barry Burn in front of the 18th green, Van de Velde chose to try to hit a 2-iron off the "fantastic" lie instead of wedging to the fairway and playing safe with the aim of making 5 or 6. Instead of, say, taking away the 2-iron and snapping it over a knee and handing his man a wedge, caddie Angiolin didn't dissent.

"I didn't feel comfortable hitting wedge," said Van de Velde, France's top player for a decade and winner of one European Tour event, in 1993. "To me that would have gone against the spirit of the game. I didn't think it was that difficult of a (2-iron) shot, so I went with it."

Van de Velde pushed the shot about 6 yards right and his Titleist turned into a pinball. The ball struck a steel railing support on the grandstand, bounced back onto the narrow top brick strip of the burn and hopped back across the burn into hay-like rough, about 40 yards from the spot it hit.

"A traumatic lie," Van de Velde said. "I would've been better off in the water."

The lie was such, he said, his only play was to go forward, and his pitch went into the burn. Van de Velde took off his shoes and socks and considered blasting the submerged ball out, but by the time he got into the burn the ball had sunk a couple of inches, he said. So he dropped, to another terrible lie back in the high rough, and pitched his fifth into the right greenside bunker. Now he needed to get up-and-down to get into a playoff, and he did so, making a 6-footer to save triple and hope.

After holing out, Van de Velde told playing partner Craig Parry, "I went for the glory and now I'm going to have to pay the price." By nightfall, after Lawrie finished birdie-birdie for even par to win the four-hole playoff by three strokes (15 to 18) over Leonard and VDV—the regretful Frenchman was in the midst of a mental mulligan.

"Next time I hit a wedge," he said, referring to the second shot. "I'm angry with myself because obviously that's not the shot to be played. I shouldn't have hit the 2-iron . . . But if I hit the 2-iron 15 feet and make the putt, people would say, 'This guy is unreal.'"

People said it anyway after the blowup, after he played the first 71 holes in 3-over par and his next two holes at 5 over. That shift in fortune devastated him a lot, he said, but he offered perspective. "There's worse things in life," said the man who sought to become the first Frenchman to win the Open since Arnaud Massy in 1907. "Some terrible things are happening to other people."

He went so far to say he had a "great week," even though he suffered the biggest last-hole demise in a major since Sam Snead made a triple-bogey 8 and finished one shot out of a playoff in the 1939 U.S. Open.

As it happened, Van de Velde's "great week" couldn't rival that of Lawrie, the introverted, 30-year-old Scot from Aberdeen. He called his good fortune a "fairy story." He made the most of a stunning gift, making birdies on the last two extra holes, Nos. 17-18, from 10 and 3 feet, respectively. The first broke a tie with Leonard after each began with two bogeys.

"Obviously Jean had the tournament in his pocket," Lawrie said after his second PGA European Tour victory of the year and third overall. "He chips it down the 18th fairway, hits it on the green, makes 5, he's the Open champion. He went for the shot. I'm not here to criticize him, though. I feel sorry for him. He really should've won. Thankfully for me he didn't."

When he finished the third round with a 76, 10 over and 10 back, Lawrie said, "I don't think I'm within range." When he finished early at plus-6, four shots behind the final two-ball's joint lead through 10 holes, Lawrie wasn't much more hopeful. "I can't see 6 over winning," he said.

But, he ended up with the farthest last-round comeback by a major winner, surpassing Jack Burke Jr.'s march from eight back in the 1956 Masters. And he finished with the highest winning total in a major (73-74-76-67=290) since Jack Nicklaus' 290 in the 1972 U.S. Open at Pebble Beach.

Lawrie ended a four-year run of American champions, a streak that included Leonard's 1997 triumph at Royal Troon. More important hereabouts, he became the first Scot to win the Open since English-born Sandy Lyle in 1985, the first Scottish-born since Tommy Armour in 1931 and the first Scottish resident since Willie Auchterlonie 106 years ago. Moreover, Lawrie was the first player in 40 years to claim the claret jug without first having won in the United States.

Lawrie's victory was so unexpected that his parents and brother went to Spain on holiday for the week and his wife stayed home with the two kids, only 40 miles up the A92 in Aberdeen.

Never in the Order of Merit top 20 since joining the European tour in 1992, Lawrie has played the role of long shot and afterthought before. He shot 4 under the last round of 36-hole Open qualifying at Downfield just to get in the Carnoustie field by two shots. He was a 150-1 starting Thursday and Sunday. Considered an underachiever by some peers, he turned pro as a 4-handicapper at 17 and eventually became a practice-range pro. He was struggling so much in the mid-1990s that he considered quitting.

But now he's on the Ryder Cup team. Now he's planning to buy a Ferrari and maybe a new house in Aberdeen. Now people will pay more attention to the sneaky-long low-ball hitter known as "Chippy" because of his chipping prowess.

Now he's thankful, not only to Van de Velde, but to Parry. The Australian known as Popeye led by one stroke with seven holes left. Parry, however, triple bogeyed the 12th when he got tangled in the hay and double bogeyed the 17th upon three-putting from 20 feet, missing from 2½ feet. One stroke hither or yon and he's in the playoff.

For the week, only Lawrie and Leonard went sans double bogey, though both flirted often. While the Barry Burn at 18 drowned Van de Velde and Leonard, Lawrie was blessed there. His approach shot on the 72nd hole skipped over the burn, and he saved par from the left bunker. Still, he had scant hope after that six-birdie 67, during which he made a 35-footer and two from 25 feet, the latter at the 71st.

Leonard, meanwhile, struggled so that he had to one-putt just for bogeys on four of his last five holes, including the play-off. He swing was off after he birdied the 14th hole of the fourth round. Twice he found the burn at 18, the first with a 3-wood from rough while trying to make birdie and cut into a two-stroke deficit.

"Basically I lost the British Open twice in one day," said Leonard, who started Sunday five back, just as he had in his three most recent victories. "Maybe it's twice as hard to take. . . . But as bad as I feel, (Van de Velde) feels worse. It had to be a sick feeling for him."

He would be correct.

But when someone told Van de Velde his T-2 earned an invitation to the 2000 Masters, his eyes brightened under an umbrella. Finally, sunshine broke through his Carnoustie gray as he thought of America, where he hopes to play full time soon, maybe next year.

"That," Jean Van de Velde said of the Masters, "is the best (expletive) news all day."

Jeff Rude is Senior Writer for Golfweek, *from which this piece is taken.*

FROM:
GOLF DREAMS

John Updike

One learns rather little watching the pros on television—
they make it look too easy, like gravity-defying computer
graphics—but earlier this year I admired a culminating shot of
Tom Kite's, in the Atlanta Classic. He had won only one tournament in nearly two years, and was said to be over the hill,
but now he had a two-shot edge. His drive was sitting up in the
short rough on the righthand side of the fairway of the eighteenth hole, a par-five with water here and there. He was on
national television. He should have been as tight as a tin man
left out in the rain; even a pro would have been forgiven for
playing up short, chipping on, and taking his winning par. But

TOM KITE

no: with that ghostly little half-smile of his, Kite plucked a wood out of the bag—a 4-wood, I think—and whipped through the ball with a swing that left the club hanging down his back and his back foot up on its toe like a ballerina's in its little pink slipper. It was picture-book fluidity, and the ball landed not only on the green 220 yards away but close enough for him to sink the putt and finish with a superfluous, superlative eagle. A lifetime of tournaments, and a certain undying joy in the game, had gone into that marvellous trust in his swing, that saintly *letting go* that golf asks of its devotees.

John Updike has lived in Massachusetts, where he took up golf, since 1957. This excerpt is from Golf Dreams, *1996.*

TIGER WOODS

TIGER WOODS, 1994 U.S. AMATEUR

Tim Rosaforte

The 1994 U.S. Amateur Championship would become a benchmark for Tiger Woods. It would define him for the first time before a national television audience, and put him in the starring role of a melodrama that Michael Crichton and George Lucas would have been hard-pressed to script. The suspense started in the semifinal round, when Tiger faced Buddy Alexander, a former U.S. Amateur champion who was coaching the University of Florida golf team. It ended with the most dramatic comeback in U.S Amateur history.

Tiger had coasted through qualifying, shooting 65 in the first round on the Stadium course and then 72 on the Valley course. In the opening round, 36-year-old PGA Tour rules official Vaughn Moise pushed him to the 17th hole, but Tiger prevailed two up. Moise called Woods a "man-child" and predicted it wouldn't be long before he was working with Woods on the PGA Tour. It wouldn't be that easy against Alexander.

The Gator golf coach was three up playing the 13th and facing a 2½-foot putt for par that would have meant a four up advantage with five holes to go—a trap not even Tiger himself could have clawed his way out of.

But Alexander left the cage door unlocked, lipping out the putt and triggering a comeback that Earl Woods predicted as he sat on his walking stick, looking like Buddha and listening to his jazz tapes. "This isn't over yet," Earl predicted. "Tiger will make another run."

It wasn't so much Tiger making another run as it was his opponent blowing all four tires. Starting with that miss at the 13th, Alexander finished bogey-bogey-bogey-bogey-bogey-double bogey. It was about as ugly as it could get. Afterward, cleaning out his locker, Alexander was exasperated. "I just played lousy and if you don't make a par from the 13th hole on, you're not going to beat anyone, no matter who he is," Alexander said.

Woods caught a huge break at the par-three 17th; when his nine-iron into the island green caught a gust of right-to-left wind and flirted with the black swamp water. Woods leaned right. His caddy and sports psychologist Jay Brunza leaned right. The ball leaned right, too, stopping eight inches from the edge of danger. Woods exhaled. Brunza exhaled. Alexander three-putted from 22 feet and threw his ball in the moat. "I was about to pass out," Woods said.

The next two matches were breathers for Woods—and he needed it. In the Round of 16 he beat Tim Jackson of Germantown, Tenn., five and four, then took care of Eric

Frishette of Carroll, Ohio, in the semifinals, five and three. Against Frishette, an All-American at Kent State, Woods played his best golf since the opening round of qualifying. Starting at No. 6, he ripped off five birdies in eight holes to steamroll into the finals giant Trip Kuehne of Oklahoma State. At the 582-yard, par-five ninth hole, he hit a 300-yard drive and a cut three-wood over the branches of a live oak tree to set up a conceded birdie. That green is rarely reached during the Players Championship, but not that many pros can fly a three-wood over 270 yards. "I could have easily reached it if I hit a hook," Woods explained. "But that would have been a dangerous shot on that hole with the woods on the left, so I played a fade, knowing that I couldn't get in any danger."

Danger was the operative word for Woods against Kuehne. He was six down after 13 holes, five down with 12 holes to play . . . and still came storming back. Kuehne, whose sister Kelli had won the U.S. Girls' Junior five weeks earlier, birdied seven of the first 13 holes, none with a putt of more than four feet, and shot 66 for a four-up lead at the lunch beak.

Earl wasn't worried. Before Tiger went out for the second 18, he whispered in his son's ear, "Let the legend grow."

Kuehne made birdie at the second to go five up again, but that was his last birdie of the match. Woods won the 4th, 7th, 9th, 10th, 11th, 16th, 17th and 18th holes. After that birdie at the second, Kuehne would win only one other hole, with a par at the sixth. It was the greatest comeback in the 99-year history of the event. And it was punctuated by Wood's fist pumping birdie at the 17th, that hellish little par-three surrounded by water and haunted by the echoing cries of Pete Dye, who designed it with double bogey in mind.

Tiger stood on that tee, having just made birdie at the 16th to even the match, holding a pitching wedge and taking practice swings as the wind did its dance in the trees. He had saved par from the woods on the 10th and 14th holes, but a miss here and there was no pine straw to catch his ball. A miss here, and Tiger was rinsed and walking to the drop circle.

The wind died and Woods grabbed a pitching wedge that was loaded with lead tape. He had 139 yards to the hole, the wind slightly at his back, and the heart of a lion thumping in his chest. His target? A stupid question. "The pin," he would say later. "I was going directly at the pin."

This was to be the friction point. The fearless tee shot landed in the Bermuda Triangle of the Sawgrass-TPC, right of the pin at the 17th. At her home in Cypress, Tida Woods rolled off her bed and onto the floor when the ball caught a piece of green, took one hop to the fringe, then spun back, no more than three feet from the water's edge. "That boy almost gave me a heart attack," Tida Woods said. "All I kept saying was, 'God, don't let that ball go into the water.' That boy tried to kill me."

It seemed as if everybody watching was holding his breath—everybody except Woods, who had faith that sand wedge was the right club and that his ball would follow its command and sit on the green. "You don't see too many pros hit it right of that pin," Kuehne said afterward. "It was a great gamble that paid off."

The ensuing putt, which dropped for birdie, was in the 14-foot range, but afterward Woods couldn't remember the distance, the break, or the grain. He couldn't even remember hitting the putt or the celebration that followed. He was too zoned out.

Walking to the 18th tee, Brunza reminded Woods to stay focused. There was big trouble down the left side, and the hole was 440 yards, but Woods was long enough to avoid the water with a two-iron. He flat-out killed it, driving it to a spot that the pros find with their drivers during the TPC. He had only a seven-iron into the green, and two-putted for the win that had the country buzzing. Earl dropped his walking stick and made his way onto the green, embracing his son as applause rained down from the spectators on the stadium mounds. It was getting to be a clichéd scene, but this was the first time it had been broadcast nationally on ESPN.

Kuehne's father (and caddy), Ernie Kuehne, called it "divine intervention." Woods said it was indescribable. Earl put it in historical perspective. "When Tiger won his first U.S. Junior [in 1991]," the old man said, "I said to him, 'Son, you have done something no black person in the United States has ever done, and you will forever be a part of history.' But this is ungodly in its ramifications."

Tim Rosaforte is a Senior Writer for Sports Illustrated *and former president of the* Golf Writers Association of America.

DAVID DUVAL

DAVID DUVAL'S 59!
(1999)

Thomas Bonk

La Quinta—It is golf's magic number—59. It's the ultimate lowdown, the most of the least, the sum total of greatness when the only thing suitable for writing it down on your scorecard is a gold pen.

For David Duval, it was his final-round score Sunday, the one that won the Bob Hope Chrysler Classic, an almost numbingly routine-looking 59 that moved him past the 12 players who began the day in front of him, allowed him to collect a $540,000 winner's check and let him walk straight into golf history.

The taciturn 27-year-old with the wraparound sunglasses left everybody else in the shadows once again. Duval, normally as emotional as granola, double-pumped his fist the moment his six-foot eagle putt disappeared into the hole at No. 18, the 59th and last of his shots, worth a two-shot lead over Steve Pate.

Four groups ahead of the lead group that included Pate, Duval waited to see if he would be caught. His lead over Pate was only one shot when Duval stood off to the side of the grandstand at No. 18 and chewed on an apple. Then he heard the groans when Pate's last chance, an 18-foot birdie putt, spun out of the hole to end it.

Of course, that's when Duval let it all hang out then.

He smiled.

For Duval, that's an eruption of emotion, but then again, shooting a 59 on the last day to win a tournament isn't your typical day, is it?

"It's like pitching a perfect game," Duval said.

And so it was. Pate deserved better since he didn't exactly roll over in a bunker and cover himself with sand. He closed with a 66 to finish at 25-under par and only lost because somebody dropped a 59 on him. This is golf's equivalent to being struck by lightning.

"I played better than everybody but one guy," Pate said. "I guess you could say I was in the wrong place at the wrong time."

Meanwhile, Duval kept up his uncanny knack of finding himself in the right place at the right time.

Add it up and it's sort of monotonous.

- Two victories in his only two starts this year.
- More than $1 million in his two weeks this year ($1,008,000).
- Nine victories in his last 28 tournaments.
- Nearly $4.9 million in prize money in the last 15 months.

So how good is this guy playing?

"I'm playing quite well," Duval said.

Yes, and desert sand is a little dry. Duval's 59 was only the third in PGA Tour history (Al Geiberger in 1977 and Chip Beck in 1991 also accomplished the feat.) He needed it all to win this time.

Duval, who began the day tied for 13th, was seven shots behind Fred Funk. Duval was 13 under par for the first 72 holes and 13 under par the last 18 holes. He birdied No. 1 at the Palmer Course on Sunday, the same hole he double-bogeyed Saturday. He shot a 28 on the back nine—which Duval also did last year at Tucson.

He had 11 birdies and an eagle to go with six pars . . . maybe he wasn't trying on those holes. He even had playing partner Jeff Maggert convinced he was playing a different course.

"I didn't know we were playing par twos today," Maggert said.

As it turned out, everyone else was playing a different game than Duval, at least for one round.

Pate won $324,000 for second and John Huston $204,000 for third after his closing 66 brought him in at 24-under 336. Funk and Bob Estes tied for fourth and Skip Kendall was sixth.

Duval produced rounds of 70-71-64-70-59 for a 26-under total of 334. It's the 59 that sort of stands out.

"What more can you say?" Pate asked. "If he doesn't jump to No. 1 in the world rankings, there's something seriously wrong."

In the meantime, there's something seriously right with Duval. He isn't particularly long and he isn't particularly big, but he is particularly successful. But Duval doesn't like to be drawn into discussions about his streak.

"I don't consider it a streak," Duval said. "Sure, I may be nine of 29 or whatever, but I'm nine for probably 120 total or something in my career. So the percentage isn't quite as baffling if you look at it that way. I prefer to look at it that way."

As for being the best player in the world, well, Duval played along to make a point.

"All right, let's say I'm the best player in the world. Great. Congratulations to me. That doesn't help me get better. It doesn't help me shoot a better score on Sunday. It doesn't do anything for me. Improving does."

No one in professional golf has ever done any better than what Duval did Sunday.

He birdied the first three holes, a nice start that included three-footers on the second and third. He tapped in for par at No. 4, then birdied the par-three 5th from five feet. He parred the next three holes, but birdied No. 9 after an eight-iron left him eight feet away.

Duval began the back with three more birdie putts, the first two from four feet and the third, at the par-three 12th, from two feet. He tapped in for par at No. 13, then birdied three more in a row. He hit a sand wedge to 10 feet on the par-five 14th, hit an eight-iron to a foot and a half of the hole at the par-three 15th and made a putt from six feet at No. 16.

He two-putted from 20 feet at the par-five 17th and then started thinking about a possible eagle at the 543-yard par-five 18th—with a 59 staring him in the face.

After his drive, Duval had 177 yards to the front of the green and 218 yards to the hole. So full of emotion, he chose a five-iron and let it go.

"Obviously, I'm a little juiced at the time," he said. "My main thought was to knock it on and have a decent putt. I wasn't positive I could get it all the way back to the hole. But it looked good all the way. I was just screaming for it to get there, and it did."

The ball stopped rolling six feet to the left of the hole. Duval read the putt, stood over the ball and rolled it in. He had his magic number.

Duval had to admit he was thinking 59 all the way, but he wasn't going to get all excited or anything. That just isn't his style.

"I took a couple of deep breaths and hit it and you just see what happens."

What happens is another entry into the record books.

Afterward, Duval had a hard time expressing his feelings about his 59.

"It is kind of a terrible thing because I am sitting here and I don't know what to tell you. I just don't. It's something that you just don't think about.

"Those kind of rounds you just couldn't go out and do. Things have to go your way."

For 18 holes and 59 shots on a Sunday in the desert, they surely went Duval's way.

Thomas Bonk's article appeared January 25, 1999 in the Los Angeles Times.

Photo Credits